Run to the Battle

by
Roberts Liardon

EMBASSY
PUBLISHING

4th Printing
35,000 in Print

Run to the Battle
ISBN 1-879993-06-6

Published by Embassy Publishing Co.
P.O. Box 3500
Laguna Hills, California 92654

Contents

Foreword

by
Karl Strader
The Carpenter's Home Church
Lakeland, Florida

Roberts Liardon is a hard-hitting young man who preaches with the maturity of a well-seasoned veteran. This book is written just like Roberts preaches. Refreshing. Simple. To the point. Anointed.

The Church, the Body of Christ, is in trouble. If the members will read this book, especially leaders in the Church, and respond, we can get well. This bold young man has sanctified brass that is needed to cut away the sham and the pretense of the average one of us.

In the coming years, the Church is going to see warfare at its highest pitch. The faint-hearted won't stand a chance. Whether young like Liardon, or old like me, we must be bold, aggressive, fervent.

This book says, "Let the weak say, I am strong!" I dare you to read it through carefully and open-heartedly. You'll never be the same.

Introduction

We are in a very interesting time, approaching the end of the second millenium since Jesus was born in Bethlehem of Judaea in the days of Caesar Augustus. Many of the prophecies and visions of the revival will begin to be fulfilled in this hour.

Some new things are going to happen in the Kingdom — powerful demonstrations of the Holy Spirit — and some of them are going to challenge a lot of people. Many things people want, God is not going to grant for a while. He is going to do a great deal more cleaning before He starts granting some of the things we want to see. We are going to see more clearly what the apostolic and the prophetic flow is for the Church.

There is going to be an acceleration. Things are going to speed up. Time is going to speed up, and time must become a friend to us rather than an enemy. The only place you can become a friend of time is in the realm of the Spirit, because if you are not in the Spirit realm, time is your enemy. Time is a controlling factor that the flesh does not like.

In the mid-Eighties, the Church began to hear about a new move of God — the former rain and the latter rain revealed to the prophet Joel. We heard about a wind of the Spirit that would bring great signs and wonders, and we got excited about God doing a powerful revival in the earth. Then everything calmed down and got real quiet. We quit singing latter rain songs, because we thought the rain had come and gone. The excitement just faded away.

But I was not satisfied in my spirit. I got on my knees and said, "God, if the latter rain came, why couldn't we tell the difference? If it came, where is all the power that was prophesied? Where are the visions and dreams? Where are the trances like the ones the Bible talks about? (Acts 10:10; 22:17.) Why aren't our hands flowing with miracle-working power? What is going on, God?"

Years earlier, God told me to study the great men and women of the past, to find out what made them great, what made them rise, and what made them fall — if they fell. In studying them, I saw what destroyed many of them was not a lack of knowledge of the Word, nor a lack of love for God, nor a lack of a desire to help people. In many cases, it was personal problems caused by demonic influence. Those demons would lie dormant until these leaders were at their height of popularity, then move in and pull them down.

Why are the miracles and power so conspicuously absent from our churches today? *Because so few people are willing to pay the price to get to the place in God where there are no strongholds for the devil to use against them.* Signs and wonders should be following us, because the Word says so. God has not changed and will not change, so obviously we are the ones who are going to have to change if we want to be a part of the revival.

We want to get out there and work *for* God without going very deep *in* God, but He is going to require that we go deep. He has rearranged a lot of schedules. He has rearranged a lot of desires. He has rearranged a lot of what people think God has told them — when He has not spoken it at all. A lot of soulish planning must be stopped and destroyed for the Church to be in prime position for the revival.

There will be more visitations and greater prophetic utterances, a scriptural characteristic of the last days. Visions belong to the young. Dreams belong to the old, according to the prophet Joel. God always "telegraphs" what He is going to do with forewarnings. He tells his prophets what He is going to do. He is going to forewarn us of our homegoing with visions or visits by certain people to heaven or hell.

> **Behold, the former things are come to pass, and new things do I declare: before they spring forth I tell you of them.**
>
> **Isaiah 42:9**

God is telling us before these things come forth in full measure. He is telling us of them through revelation and through demonstrations that are the first fruits of the revival.

Yes, God is doing something new, but we have to get ready for it. Then as soon as we are ready, we have to jump into it, because it is already moving. It is not coming at some vague time in the future. *It is here now.*

God also is beginning to unveil the leadership of the revival that has come into the earth. We are going to see new leaders come, and many of them are going to be young in age but not in spiritual maturity. Young people have a divine destiny in this hour, and it is not to run the normal course of life. There is a greater call.

Sometimes I look at the few new leaders who have been brought out, and I think, "Lord, who else are you going to put into position?"

I looked at someone and thought, "Well. . . might work over there," and the Lord said, "There is a whole new group you do not even know about."

I just want to meet them!

We have seen the hour of the teacher. The teaching office will not be the dominant anointing in the future. I am not saying that there are no more teachers. Teachers will never disappear; however, there will come *preachers* to blast into the revival. They will cause a great disturbance in the realm of the Spirit, and they will reap a harvest that we have been foreseeing and prophesying about.

This move of God is different from most of the past moves. Man did not have to work very hard to receive them. The Spirit did most of it. Man did not have to strive very hard to be part of the Voice of Healing move, or the Word of Faith move, or the Charismatic move. Of course there was intercession and conflict and trial and persecution involved, particularly for the leaders. But most of the average believers needed very little effort to be part of those moves.

However, this move involves individual effort, because holiness is such a big part of it. You cannot just slide into this move. This one takes individual commitment. This one demands change in spirit, soul and body.

Jesus said, **For unto whomsoever much is given, of him shall be much required** (Luke 12:48). No other generation has been given as much scripture and as much revelation as this one. God is requiring more of us. He will not allow us to quote scriptures like a machine gun, then go out and commit adultery. This is not a day of cheap grace. Judgment has already begun in the house of the Lord.

Many people are not living in the realm of the Holy Spirit. They are out there running around with familiar spirits, having visions that come from some place other than heaven. The Lord gave many of us a mandate to deal with these things in a very bold and plain way, because we are not facing a generation that understands hints. They will not listen. Things must be said by the Holy Spirit in a way to get their attention boldly.

Living in the realm of the Holy Spirit — in the realm of miracles and power — is not like running in a hundred-yard dash with its quick sprint and emotional high. No, it is more like a marathon. The only way you are going to win this race is to decide to run no matter what comes and no matter what goes. It takes commitment to stay in there and keep putting one foot in front of the other.

It is time to get ready for the new move and time to get into it. If you want to be part of the revival, this book will help you get ready. It will help you press into that place in God where the supernatural is natural.

1

His Calling Voice Comes Again

The calling voice of God comes to every generation questioning and searching for the response that brings divine satisfaction.

In the Garden of Eden, His voice rang out, **Where art thou?** (Gen. 3:9.)

In Abraham's day, God was calling for separation unto Him. (Gen. 12:1.)

In Samuel's first years as a child ministering to the Lord before Eli, God was calling for holiness in the priests so that His Spirit might be restored in the tabernacle. (1 Sam. 3.)

In Ezekiel's time, God was calling for an intercessor, one to stand in the gap between His mercy and judgment, one to call for His grace. (Ezek. 22:30.)

In Nehemiah's generation, God's voice called for restoration, for the city of Jerusalem to be rebuilt and for the nation of Judah to be restored as a people. (Neh. 13:5.)

Today, God's voice is calling to us as it did in the days of Samuel. He is calling for holiness in His "temples" (His children) in order for the moving of the Holy Spirit to grow stronger.

So many churches are standing far from the shore of Holy Spirit revival. They are fooled by *material*

9

success into thinking they have achieved *spiritual* success. Where they once desired spiritual meat, now they eat from the minds of men — soul "junk food." The hunger of God's people for spiritual food must be answered by the leadership today.

Yes, we preachers will be held accountable for such action. You may think I am being harsh or critical; however, I am not being judgmental — I am simply stating facts and including myself in the warning.

Many spiritual leaders will stand in the Judgment and desire to have another opportunity to answer the Lord's call of:

"Who will stand and bring the soul-led and sin-bound church of the Eighties into the roaring winds of the Nineties as Samuel brought Israel from spiritual decay to a tremendous revival?"

His calling voice is coming to us today with strength, even as a roar. Let us humble ourselves before Him and help a needy generation. Let Jesus be seen instead of ourselves so that He may walk again among His people and answer their desires.

God Is Calling Those Who Will Hear and Obey

Today's situation is similar to the days of Samuel.

> **And the child Samuel ministered unto the Lord before Eli. And the word of the Lord was precious (valuable because it was scarce) in those days; there was no open vision.**
>
> **And it came to pass at that time, when Eli was laid down in his place, and his eyes began to wax dim, that he could not see;**

> And ere the lamp of God went out in the temple of the Lord, where the ark of God was, and Samuel was laid down to sleep;
>
> That the Lord called Samuel: and he answered, Here am I.
>
> And he ran unto Eli, and said, Here am I; for thou calledst me. And he said, I called not; lie down again. And he went and lay down.
>
> And the Lord called yet again, Samuel. And Samuel arose and went to Eli, and said, Here am I; for thou didst call me. And he answered, I called not, my son; lie down again.
>
> Now Samuel did not yet know the Lord, neither was the word of the Lord yet revealed unto him.
>
> And the Lord called Samuel again the third time. And he arose and went to Eli, and said, Here am I; for thou didst call me. And Eli perceived that the Lord had called the child.
>
> **1 Samuel 3:1-8**

Eli was supposed to be a great prophet. He was the high priest for all of Israel, the one who ministered to the Lord before the Ark of the Covenant. He was supposed to hear God and lead His people in the ways God commanded. Yet Eli's home was a mess, and today many prophets' homes are a mess.

The sons of Eli, who served as priests under his authority, were fornicating at the doors of the temple! They were stealing and doing all sorts of evil, and Eli did not have the backbone to compel them to change. He admonished them, but he did not speak with the authority of a father or a high priest. If a man cannot rebuke his own sons, how is he going to confront God's people who are going the wrong way and bring the needed correction?

Also in our day, there is no open vision — which in the original means "very little." I am not saying no miracles happen today. But if we really *heard and obeyed* the Holy Spirit, there would be a consistent flow of miracles. Not many people know the voice of God; their "perceivers" are rusty, like Eli's.

The reason the "perceivers" of many Christians are inoperative is because they are trying to function in the realm of the Spirit with their minds — and that will not work. They have a lot of "head-knowledge" about the Bible which does them little good. They do not have hearts full of the Word, but heads full of pride and religious information. The Word planted in the heart is what bears fruit.

Once I was viewing a fine-tuned ministry of helps. I believe in this ministry and see the great need for it, so *please, please* hear my heart in this. But the Spirit of the Lord spoke to me so strongly that it was like a roar:

"Excellence of ministry they have; excellence of spirit they have not."

Those words still echo in my heart. One of my board members put it so well: high gloss versus real substance.

Ministers have been so concerned over "image," the way they are perceived by the world, that they spend more of their time developing outward aspects of their ministry than their relationships with the Lord. Will a marketable image in the world's sight bring the harvest in for Jesus? Certainly not!

Then there are those who are so concerned over spiritual excesses they cannot see where the real excesses are — they cannot see the forest for the trees. They are trying to keep God's people in low gear in order to monitor every little sign of supernatural manifestation, but where are the sermons that expose excesses of soulish activity in the Church? That should be our priority. It is better to have some spiritual "wild fire" than no fire at all! A minister who will allow Jesus to flow through him will bring or win his generation to the Lord.

We Must Operate on God's Terms

John the Baptist came into *all* the country delivering God's perfect prophetic Word, regardless of who it hit and regardless of who received the Word and who did not. His only concern was the Word, and he did not allow people's feelings to weaken his message or adjust his position. He operated on God's terms, not man's.

The Lord convicted me one evening as I was preaching. There was a strong prophetic anointing, and the words that were coming up out of my spirit were so exact that they were dividing soul from spirit. (Heb. 4:12.) I began to feel a wave of actual opposition coming toward me in the pulpit.

I was shocked. To be honest, it scared me. I knew the people to whom I was speaking so well, I could not believe the reaction I was getting. I began to translate God's words into my own choice of words to lessen the blow of the opposition I felt. I changed His words to those I thought were less "offensive," but my words did not carry the same weight as those the Lord used.

John the Baptist spoke the Lord's words exactly. His message angered the leaders of his day, and so it will be in ours.

That evening, the Holy Spirit quickly rebuked me.

He said, "Who are you to change my words and make them attractive to the soul. My words bring separation and clarity to the hungry and conviction to others. Don't be afraid of that which you feel. Speak as you are spoken to."

John the Baptist said, Jesus **must increase, but I must decrease** (John 3:30).

Are we willing to say that and mean it?

The Message to Laodicea

The message to the church at Laodicea could very well have been written to many churches today.

> **Behold, I stand at the door, and knock: if any man hear my voice, and open the door, I will come in to him, and will sup with him, and he with me.**
> **Revelation 3:20**

Is Jesus standing at the door of your life and ministry trying to get in? Is Jesus allowed to move as He wills in your church? There are so many preachers today whose churches are based on their personalities. They have built followings on their personalities. Many are diverting the attention of the sheep from the Chief Shepherd to themselves.

Yes, there is always personality involved, because God works in cooperation with His children. But He wants them to be so conformed to the image of His dear Son that their characters are like that of Jesus.

On the other hand, many great leaders do try to warn people not to follow them but look at Jesus, yet some of the sheep insist — against warnings — on keeping their eyes on the men. Idolatry is one of man's greatest temptations. Idolatry is putting anything between you and Jesus. It might be money or possessions, spouse or children, or spiritual leaders, but if your focus and greatest love is on that instead of the Lord, you are verging on idolatry.

John the Baptist had a strong personality to the point that the Bible even records the kind of clothes he wore. However, what stirred the country was not his fashion in clothes or his personality, *but his message*. He subordinated his personality so the Word of the Lord could be heard and seen.

He was decreasing after Jesus began His ministry, in order for Jesus to increase. He did the best he could to get out of the limelight. Let us take an example from him. Do not build an empire where Jesus cannot be number one. Build your ministry on Jesus and not on yourself.

No more "Hollywood" preaching business, no more being concerned more over offerings than the messages, no more building ministries on something other than Jesus. Let us commit to working for God on His terms.

Notice who God spoke to when He decided it was time to do something about Eli and his wicked sons: It was a little boy whose mother cried out one day and said, "God, I need a son. If You will give me a son, I will give him back to You to serve You all the days of his life."

We Must Be Able To Hear

God answered her prayer, and when Samuel was weaned, his mother brought him to Eli to serve the Lord as she had promised. Samuel grew in the grace of the Lord and found joy in serving the old prophet. He was a simple little boy who loved God.

When the calling voice of God came to Samuel, he did not recognize it, because the voice of the Lord was not heard around the tabernacle anymore. This was something new to him. When he heard his name called, it was usually Eli telling him to do something. So three times when he heard, "Samuel, Samuel," he went running to Eli, who finally realized the Lord must be speaking.

Therefore Eli said unto Samuel, Go, lie down: and it shall be, if he call thee, that thou shalt say, Speak, Lord; for thy servant heareth. So Samuel went and lay down in his place.

And the Lord came, and stood, and called as at other times, Samuel, Samuel. Then Samuel answered, Speak; for thy servant heareth.

And the Lord said to Samuel, Behold, I will do a thing in Israel, at which both the ears of every one that heareth it shall tingle.

In that day I will perform against Eli all things which I have spoken concerning his house: when I begin, I will also make an end.

For I have told him that I will judge his house for ever for the iniquity which he knoweth; because his sons made themselves vile, and he restrained them not.

And therefore I have sworn unto the house of Eli, that the iniquity of Eli's house shall not be purged with sacrifice nor offering for ever.

And Samuel lay until the morning, and opened the doors of the house of the Lord. And Samuel feared to shew Eli the vision.

Then Eli called Samuel, and said, Samuel, my son. And he answered, Here am I.

And he said, What is the thing that the Lord hath said unto thee? I pray thee hide it not from me: God do so to thee, and more also, if thou hide any thing from me of all the things that he said unto thee.

And Samuel told him every whit, and hid nothing from him. And he said, It is the Lord: let him do what seemeth him good.

1 Samuel 3:9-18

Samuel was nervous about telling Eli what the Lord had said, but he was obedient and repeated the message exactly. He did not try to interpret it or soften it; he gave it straight. And Eli confirmed that the Lord indeed had spoken.

And Samuel grew, and the Lord was with him, and did let none of his words fall to the ground.

And all Israel from Dan even to Beersheba knew that Samuel was established to be a prophet of the Lord.

1 Samuel 3:19,20

Samuel was confirmed as a prophet of the Lord while he was still young. God is not waiting for an education. God is not waiting for a big bank account. He is not waiting for you to get to a certain age or a certain place.

God is not looking for mental agreement, but for a heart that will say, "Speak on. I'll listen. I'll obey You. I'm Your servant."

Who Will Answer the Call?

The calling voice of God is saying, "I need someone who will stand up against the flow of this world, against the pride, lethargy, and fakery in the Church, and say 'No!' I am looking for those who will be carriers of the glory of the Lord in the earth today."

God is calling those who will do what He says when He says, and not ask why. He needs generals in His army. He needs sergeants to train the rank and file. He needs captains who will stand up against the stubbornness of some Church leaders, against laziness in some pews.

He is looking for those who will confront the sons of Eli and say, "This is the way the Lord says we shall go, and if you don't go this way, what comes to you is your own fault."

This journey cannot be made with your flesh untouched. Romans 8:8 says, **So then they that are in the flesh cannot please God.** Flesh must be under divine control from your spirit man. The Church must come back into the realm of the Spirit, the realm of real faith. God does not need any more hype. He does not need any more soulish ministry masquerading as spiritual. The things of the flesh must be cut off and exposed, allowing the truth to come forth.

God is giving a fresh anointing to those who will receive it. His voice is going through every home and every church in the world. His voice is going to every ear in the world — saint or sinner — and His voice is being heard, whether it is recognized or not. It is heard by young and by old.

God's voice is not asking what you know but saying, "Are you willing. Are you willing? Will you yield your life to me? Will you give up the things of this world — the weights and the anchors of this world — and come away with Me? Come into the Spirit realm that I have made for you. I will carry you and show you the glory I have waiting for you."

This revival of God has come into the earth, and it has come as close as it is going to come. For this one, we must reach up and turn loose of all the weights and anchors. We must begin to journey.

We must travel without looking back, without saying, "Lord, my friends aren't coming. My relatives aren't coming."

We cannot look at all of these people. We must look unto the Author and Finisher of our faith, and journey closer to Him to go higher and go wider. Remain in the truth that you have learned, but never stay behind. Many men and women are missing their visitations from heaven, because they are not following the voice of the Lord but some man or some doctrine that will not stand in the fire of God.

Remember, there are no excuses in God's court. You cannot say you are too young or too old, or you do not know enough, or you do not have enough time. Open your heart and allow God to put within you the ability, the grace, to be established in the earth. He will give you the ability and the strength to do what He has called you to do.

Then the world will stand back and say, "Who are you, and where did you come from?"

And you will be able to reply, "I am a man (or woman) of God, and I got here with the ability of God not of men."

One evening the Lord spoke this prophecy:

The ability of God shall rise up out of you, and you shall hear with your own ears the voice of the Lord coming out, and you will learn as you speak. You will learn as I begin to flow out of you, because that is one of the greatest schools that I have implemented in the Church — the school of My Spirit. Men may say and men may do, but my Spirit knows it all.

So this day, lean not on your own understanding and lean not to the right or to the left, nor to the front nor to the back, but look up and go that way. For the calling voice of God is coming and has come unto you, and you must learn that when you answer that call, and when you begin to journey on this road to a higher place and higher realm that all hell will try to stop you. But understand this: The gates of hell shall not prevail against the Kingdom of God that is within you!

2

Are You Ready
To Subdue Kingdoms?

And what more shall I say? For time will fail me
if I tell of Gideon, Barak, Samson, Jephthah, of David
and Samuel and the prophets.

Who by faith conquered kingdoms, performed
acts of righteousness, obtained promises, shut the
mouths of lions,

Quenched the power of fire, escaped the edge of
the sword, from weakness were made strong, became
mighty in war, put foreign armies to flight.
Hebrews 11:32-34 NAS

God gave us faith so we could conquer or subdue
kingdoms and bring righteousness. We are supposed
to overcome kingdoms and bring them into submission
to the hand or will of God. (Matt. 6:10.)

When I got back from my 1984 trip to Africa, the
Lord kept bringing the phrase **who subdued kingdoms**
(Heb. 11:33) to me. I have studied church history for
many years and read about preachers who could take
communities or cities. Some could take several cities
in one move, while others could take a whole nation.
The Bible records a number of people who were
subduers of nations.

Not long ago, I returned from a preaching tour in
Europe — and the Christians in Europe are doing great!
It is no longer where darkness rules. The light has

21

begun to shine. What God is doing in Europe and other nations is wonderful, and what He is doing in our country is wonderful. The United States is not going under, not if we answer the calling voice of God in our generation.

God did not call us to hide in a corner. He called us to be bold out in the open, to make people nervous in a positive way as John the Baptist did, and to say what the Holy Spirit says.

He did not call us to try to keep from offending anyone. We need to understand that when we got saved, we enlisted in an army. If you are a part of the Body of Christ, you are in some degree of spiritual warfare. God did not call us to tolerate the devil and his works. He called us to destroy the works of the devil.

Look at Gideon for an example:

> **And the angel of the Lord appeared unto him, and said unto him, The Lord is with thee, thou mighty man of valour.**
>
> **Judges 6:12**

Like most of us, the "mighty man of valour" did not believe that he was like that. At the time the angel appeared, he was hiding some of his produce from the Midianites, because they had overrun the land. Gideon wanted to know why the enemies of Israel had run over them *if the Lord truly was with them.*

That is what many of us are saying. "If God truly is with us, why are all these things happening?" The answer is the same as then: These things happen because the enemy — Midianites in Gideon's day, the devil in ours — has not been pushed out of our territory.

Revival is a divine attack on Satan's rule in society. We are called to invade every aspect of satanic influence. God never called His Church to go out and take people out of the world and put them in a quiet little corner, saying, "Now stay there until Jesus comes."

Jesus never meant for us to look at the Rapture as an escape route. When He returns, we are to be found working and *occupying.* He did not call us to hide and be silent. When He returns, we ought to be busy obeying His directions, which may be building new churches, putting new ministries on television and radio, writing new books, or moving out in new evangelistic campaigns around the world.

The Lord Is a Fighter

The Lord is a warrior. He is a fighter. Today, we desperately need a revelation of that part of His character. For so long, Jesus was presented as a sort of "wimpy" meek-and-mild man, when He really was the opposite. He had to be bold and assertive to walk through the religious society and the civil structure of His day. He was concerned with speaking only what His Father said, and not with the reactions of men.

Gideon's second question was:

> ...And where be all his miracles which our fathers told us of, saying, Did not the Lord bring us up from Egypt? but now the Lord hath forsaken us, and delivered us into the hands of the Midianites.
> **Judges 6:13**

Many Christians are looking at their towns and cities and saying, "When is God going to move? Where are all of the miracles our fathers told us of in generations past?"

God is waiting for Gideons. When He finds someone who will be a Gideon, He will move. The Lord looked at Gideon and said *go*. He did not say to sit down and talk, or to wait for a better time.

He said, "Gideon, you go and save Israel from the hand of the Midianites."

Gideon had a lot of excuses, just as we have: His family was poor, and among his family, he was "the least." He was afraid. But God did not accept his excuses. He did not feel sorry for Gideon and go find someone else.

God said, "I will be with you, and you can smite them *as one man*." (Judg. 6:16.)

You can be a one-man army. That is what the great spiritual leaders of the past were. When Billy Sunday came to town, the saloons went out of business. We must come out of our "accommodation-with-the-world" thinking.

Love has two sides: unconditional *acceptance* and divine *confrontation*. Unconditional *permissiveness* is not love. "Sloppy agape" is not love. "Cheap grace" is not love. When Jesus cleansed the temple, He did not walk in there nicely and politely ask the moneychangers to leave. No, He strode in there with a whip in His hand and truth on His lips. He loudly spoke out the will of the Father. If that happened in our day, a lot of church people would say Jesus was arrogant, rude, and "not walking in love!"

God is bringing a more balanced understanding of the love walk. This generation, which came to adulthood in the rebellious atmosphere of the Sixties, has mistaken *love* for *license,* for the freedom to do whatever is right in its own sight.

Jesus Taught How To Confront Evil

Jesus went about doing good — healing the sick, delivering the oppressed, and teaching the poor. He did not teach them how to "cope with life." He taught them how to confront evil, not compromise with it. Too many preachers today want to say, "Let's walk in love," and ignore the other side of love, which is divine confrontation.

The Lord gave me a vision once of many crippled and otherwise handicapped people. I was excited, thinking that a great miracle ministry had come to me.

Then the Lord said, "That's not what I am showing you. These are spiritual handicaps, spiritual conditions. These things come because My people do not know how to fight. Go to the churches where I open doors, and do not be just a teacher. Be a commander and a trainer! Show them how to fight the devil and enjoy it. My Church is in warfare. You are not there to live casually. You are in a deep battle with eternal purposes."

The warfare, the spiritual conflicts God has for us to be involved in, cannot be done in a corner. (Acts 26:26.) Paul was a militant man, and we must be militant in our day. Warfare, revival — the divine attack on society — in any day is not done in a corner. God said it is done out in the open for all to hear and receive.

We must move from fighting the devil defensively, or just to survive, to fighting him offensively, taking back territory and attacking the gates of hell. When I come into a city or a nation, I look out the airplane window on the way down and begin to pray for the people there and to bind the principalities that rule over the people there.

You have to live that way in God's army. You have to know that every place the sole of your foot touches is yours and God's. Isaiah 11:9 says the earth will be filled with the knowledge of God. And that knowledge is not going to come trickling down, but it will be as the waters that cover the sea. We are going to be the carriers of it. We are called to stir up the world, to turn it upside down (Acts 17:6), not to breeze through the world being pleasant, nice Christians.

God does not always call you to a place you like. Sometimes that is to keep you from getting caught up in the leisure activities of that place. If you are not caught up in the scenery, you will be quicker to do the bidding of the Lord. He sent me to the north, and I am a southerner. Weather in the north is not exciting to me. It snows hard and gets cold!

The Lord said, "I want you to fight the principalities of the north," and I said, "But what about the principalities of the south — like Florida?"

The principalities of my hometown, Tulsa, are not as strong as other places. They have been beaten up real good and do not move as they used to move. The demonic power is not as strong as it is other places. However, wherever we are, our fight is against principalities and demonic forces, not against other men.

> **For we wrestle not against flesh and blood, but against principalities, against powers, against the rulers of the darkness of this world, against spiritual wickedness in high places.**
>
> **Ephesians 6:12**

The warrior attitude is: Never give up. When Elisha asked God to open the eyes of his servant to see that there was more help on their side than on the enemy's, the servant saw a ring of warring angels. They had swords in their hands, not harps. (2 Kings 6:16,17.)

Some time ago, God began to speak to me that this is the season for men and women to subdue nations, bring righteousness, and obtain His promises. Too many of us look at a city and see its might, but this is not the day to be satisfied with cities. It is time that we begin to look at countries, to look at the impossibilities and grin. We can grin because we know we are going to win!

It Is Time To Subdue Nations

Of course there is a fight. We need to be forceful to subdue kingdoms. Matthew 11:12 says, **the kingdom of heaven suffereth violence, and the violent take it by force.** The *New International Version* translates it as: **the kingdom of heaven has been forcefully advancing, and forceful men lay hold of it.** Another translates it as: **they are pressing into the Realm of heaven — these eager souls are storming it!** (Mof)

The first key to subduing kingdoms is obedience. We have to learn to obey the voice of God. One reason so many believers have never been able to succeed is because they have not learned to be obedient to God.

When I was eleven years old, God called me to preach. He said, "Will you preach for me today?"

I said, "God, I haven't even finished high school yet."

He said, "If you'll follow Me and start preaching, I'll give you an education that you wouldn't receive anywhere else."

I said, "God, I'll go. I'll do it. I don't care what You want me to do, where You want me to go, or what You want me to say when I get there, I'll do it."

The First Key Is Obedience

In 1983, God said, "I want you to go to Moscow this year."

I said, "I want to go to some other nation in Europe, God."

"I don't want you to go to some other nation in Europe. You have got to go to Moscow."

"What in the world for?"

He told me to be quiet and go.

"If you want me to go," I said, "You just cause it." He did. He sent the money and had two ministers invite me to go with them. I did not want to go to Russia, but I chose to accept the desire God placed inside me. When I accepted the desire, it began to be fun, and I moved into the joy of the Lord.

We flew to Helsinki, Finland, where we met with people who were arranging our contacts inside Russia. That evening, we flew into Moscow. When we crossed the border between Finland and Russia, we did not need an announcement from the pilot. We knew it, because we could feel the liberty of the demonic spirits there.

If you are going to subdue a nation, you have to go behind enemy lines and attack from that side. You have to be cunning and wise in the Spirit, because there is a battleground out there. Do not even try it if you are not sure you can hear the voice of the Lord, or if you are not willing to be obedient.

God spoke to us during dinner and said, "This night you go to Red Square and prophesy to the walls."

I thought, "Lord, You know that is not supposed to be done — especially by American tourists."

He said, "You go, and I will tell you what to do."

When we got to our hotel, our bodies were suffering from jet lag and screaming for bed, but our spirits kept saying, "Go, go, go!" We yielded to the Spirit, and God said, "Get on the subway."

None of us could read a dab of Russian, and there are not too many people on the streets at night who can speak English, but our group obediently took the subway to Red Square. There the Spirit of God began to speak to us to prophesy to the walls.

The Lord said, "You walk that square seven times. Seven times you walk, and you prophesy. You prophesy to the red star. You prophesy and send my angels into the place where the president works."

We went to an underground church and talked with a man involved in the underground press in one region of Russia. Over lunch at his home, he shared what was happening among God's people behind the Iron Curtain. I believe Russia will see a great revival.

The Second Key: The Power of Prayer

The second key to subduing nations is learning the power of prayer. When you get down on your knees and open yourself in prayer for God to move through you, you must be totally yielded to have perfect success. You must learn how to pray without quitting. Nice little prayers will not move you into the realm where devils quake and mountains move. They will not get you to that place where signs and wonders flow. You must hook up to the vast power of God and persevere until the victory is won.

The devil declares war on you when you get into prayer.

He assigns special warriors to come against you. He does things to cause you to stop praying. If he can keep believers from praying, he has the world in his control.

You cannot just walk in and go through a religious routine. The demons will say, "Ha, ha, ha. We're not budging. You are."

The name of Jesus is powerful, but you have to enforce it. You have to hit the devils with it. You have to fight them with His most excellent name.

If you take the attitude, "I'm going to win or die fighting," the devils will be afraid of you and flee when you come on the scene.

God gave me a clear picture of the kinds of battles that are taking place for whole nations when I was flying into Zimbabwe some time ago.

God said, "Come up hither, and let me take you to a battle." He pulled me up into the Spirit realm and took me to a place where I could see the fighting without being involved in the battle.

He said, "I want you to view it before we go into it. This is the battle for the nation of Zimbabwe."

I had seen battles for individuals, for families, for financial situations and for ministries, but this was the first time I had ever seen a real battle where angels and devils were fighting directly. I saw huge, powerful creatures out there going around and around with huge, powerful angels. I saw them fighting, wrestling, and warring on the battlefield.

We have to bring down the demonic princes over cities and nations. We have to hit the devil when he tries to walk up to us. Do not wait for him to hit you first. Sock it to him. Be determined to win, to do something for God.

I do not understand believers who just pray a little bit, read a little bit, go to church a little bit, socialize a little bit, hit a little bit, forgive a little bit, and do the whole thing over. They are of little use to the Kingdom — just more numbers. Then they wonder why they never experience God, why they cannot hear the voice of the Lord.

We must learn to move in the realm of the Spirit. When God called me, I committed to be obedient and to pray. The Lord tested my obedience in many little things before he brought me to the bigger things, and I spent hour upon hour in prayer that changed me and changed things in the Spirit realm.

The trip to Russia was one of the big tests of obedience, but an even bigger test was when God told me to go to Africa.

Obedience Brings Victory and Blessings

For some time before God first began to speak to me about going to Zimbabwe, the word *Zimbabwe* would come out when I was praying in tongues. I just thought it was another word in the prayer language and did not pay any attention to it, until someone who had been praying with me said, "Did you know that Zimbabwe is a nation?"

I said, "No, where is it?"

"I don't know. I just know it is a nation."

I bought a world map and pinned it on the wall to look for Zimbabwe. When I got to the continent of Africa, the nation of Zimbabwe enlarged itself about twenty times, and the only thing I could see was Zimbabwe.

And God said, "Roberts, you are going to have to go to Zimbabwe the year you graduate from high school."

"God, I don't want to go to Zimbabwe," I said. "I want to go to Europe or some place civilized. You sent me to Moscow. It was nice, but it wasn't great."

He said, "You are going to go."

"You'll have to make it happen, or I won't go," I said. I did not give it much thought until God brought a man up to me at a convention in St. Louis.

"God spoke to me to invite you to come to my country this year," he said.

I said, "Well, all right, I will go."

After I agreed and accepted the desire for the African trip, God began to show me what to do.

"You go to Rome, and you go to the Vatican," He said. "I want you to stay there a few hours."

I thought, "God, how do You arrange that with a flight schedule?"

"Just tell them that you want to go to Uganda as well."

"Why in the world do You want me to go to Uganda as well?"

He told me to be quiet and go.

I called a travel agent and told him what I needed. He checked his computer and said it worked out perfectly. He booked our team on a flight to Rome with a thirteen-hour layover before flying to Uganda for six days, then on to Zimbabwe.

A few days after graduation, we took off for Rome.

So I went to the Vatican and walked and prophesied. I went inside and walked and prophesied, until my spirit said, "You've done enough. Now go to the airport."

Then we went to Uganda.

God said, "I'll take you from the bottom of the nation to the top of the nation."

One of our team members, Akkiki Muyu, grew up in Uganda, but had attended Oral Roberts University. She introduced us to a Full Gospel banker she knew.

We were having a nice visit when the banker leaned back in his big chair and said, "I believe you need to see the president."

"I think I do, too," I said, but I thought he was joking.

"Do you want me to call him?"

"Sure."

He picked up the phone and called the president!

"We have some American missionaries here who have been praying for you. You need to see them," he said.

So we went to the president's office. I was a little nervous, because I had never met a president of a nation before.

I was praying, "God, You're going to have to help me. What am I going to say to him, God?"

The Lord said, "Remember when I called you to preach? I told you to open up your mouth, and I would fill it. You do the same here. There is no difference."

After President Obote and I exchanged greetings and were seated, the Spirit of prophecy fell on me. I have learned that when God starts moving, no matter who you are with, you had better go with Him. If you do not, you will be in a bad predicament. No matter how strange it may look, go with God, and everything will work out. So I began to let the words boil up out of me.

"If you'll run your nation the right way, righteously before God, the nation will prosper and will grow. If you do not run the nation righteously, judgment will come. Great disaster will be upon your land. God has sent me from America to pray for you, to ask God to send His angels to be beside you, to help you."

Time Is Short

It is time to begin to expand our vision and subdue nations — in fact, it is past time. Cities and regions are not enough. However, in order for us to move into that realm of the Spirit, we must learn to obey, we must learn to pray, we must learn to yield ourselves to God, we must learn to give up the things of the world. If God calls you to do something, forget everything else and give all your strength and might to that one thing.

The day is coming, and it is not far off, when there will be nations subdued by people of God, nations that have wrought righteousness and obtained the promises. There will be nations where devils have been driven out, and the ones who refused to go are bound so tightly no one will notice them. There will be nations where you will be able to feel the mighty rushing wind of the Spirit as soon as you step across the border.

Great things will happen in our day if the people of God — especially the young evangelists — will go out and subdue the nations through faith in God and by His supernatural power.

3

The Anointing Is for Action

And it shall come to pass in that day, that his burden shall be taken away from off thy shoulder, and his yoke from off thy neck, and the yoke shall be destroyed because of the anointing.

Isaiah 10:27

The anointing destroys or breaks the yoke of bondage. The yoke of poverty is *destroyed* by the anointing. The yoke of sickness is *destroyed* by the anointing. Whatever the devil tries to put on us or send against us is destroyed by the anointing.

The anointing is not something spooky, and it is not only for full-time ministers. The anointing is for the entire Body of Christ, so we need to put aside all the weird ideas we may have about it and learn to walk in it in the practical operation of our everyday lives.

There is no Hollywood in heaven, and there are no superstars in heaven. We are *all* called to be a particular part of the Body of Christ and to flow together as one, but we cannot do it without the anointing. However, the anointing and understanding of the anointing is sadly lacking in the Church today.

What is the anointing? *The anointing is the divine power God grants to a believer through the Holy Spirit to minister to the world and the Body of Christ.*

There are many different types of anointings, but there is only one Holy Spirit.

37

> Now there are diversities of gifts, but the same Spirit.
>
> And there are differences of administrations, but the same Lord.
>
> And there are diversities of operations, but it is the same God which worketh all in all.
>
> But the manifestation of the Spirit is given to every man to profit withal.
>
> 1 Corinthians 12:4-7

Jesus is our example of ministering under the anointing. You may say, "Well, Jesus was the Son of God." That is true, but Jesus did not minister on the earth as the Son of God. He ministered as a man anointed by the Holy Spirit — the same thing He has called us to do.

Jesus laid aside everything connected with being the Son of God and operated as a mere man whose power and authority came through the Holy Spirit. He would not need to be anointed if He were ministering as the Son of God.

> Let this mind be in you, which was also in Christ Jesus:
>
> Who, being in the form of God, thought it not robbery to be equal with God:
>
> But made himself of no reputation, and took upon him the form of a servant, and was made in the likeness of men:
>
> And being found in fashion as a man, he humbled himself, and became obedient unto death, even the death of the cross.
>
> Philippians 2:5-8

The *King James Version* may be a little difficult to understand here when it says He **made himself of no reputation**. The *New American Standard Bible* translates verse 7 as: **but emptied Himself, taking the form of a bondservant, and being made in the likeness of men.** Jesus emptied Himself of His own power and submitted Himself to the will of the Father as a bondservant.

Jesus Was Anointed for Action

The Bible records the beginning of Jesus' earthly ministry in Luke 3,4. Jesus went to John the Baptist to be baptized, and as Jesus prayed **the heaven was opened, And the Holy Ghost descended in a bodily shape like a dove upon him** (Luke 3:21,22). The Holy Spirit then led Jesus into the wilderness for a forty-day fast, and He was tempted of the devil. Using the Word of God as a weapon, Jesus resisted all that the enemy sent against Him to try to stop His ministry.

> And Jesus returned in the power of the Spirit. . . .
>
> And he came to Nazareth, where he had been brought up: and, as his custom was, he went into the synagogue on the sabbath day, and stood for to read.
>
> And there was delivered unto him the book of the prophet Esaias (Isaiah). And when he had opened the book, he found the place where it was written,
>
> The Spirit of the Lord is upon me, because he hath *anointed* me to preach the gospel to the poor; he hath sent me to heal the brokenhearted, to preach deliverance to the captives, and recovering of sight to the blind, to set at liberty them that are bruised,
>
> To preach the acceptable year of the Lord.
> **Luke 4:14,16-19**

Verses 18 and 19 show what Jesus was anointed to do:

- To preach the Gospel to the poor.

- To heal the brokenhearted.

- To preach deliverance to the captives.

- To preach recovering of sight to the blind.

- To set at liberty them that are bruised.

- To preach the acceptable year of the Lord.

Notice that each item begins with a verb — an action word. *Jesus was anointed for action. He was a man of bold action.* Jesus was not anointed to take a defensive posture. Each of the actions listed was a bold thrust against the enemy. Each was an offensive move to drive the enemy out of the lives of God's people.

What is *the Gospel to the poor?* They do not have to be poor anymore! There is an anointing that will go right into poor people that will begin to lift them and break the yoke of poverty over them. This anointing works anywhere in the world. It is not just a North American Gospel. It is the Gospel of the Kingdom of God. When the poor are taught to give, God will bless them, and the spirits of poverty and lack will be driven out of their lives as well as out of entire regions.

Healing the brokenhearted does not mean joining them in a pity-party. Healing comes when things are boldly dealt with, even if it hurts. If an arm or leg needs stitches, it will hurt in the beginning but be a blessing in the long run. Jesus was compassionate but bold in dealing with the source of the problem. He cast out spirits of self-pity, grief and sorrow.

What is *preaching deliverance to captives?* The Lord showed me a vision once of people in a cage. All of them had weird smiles.

The Lord said, "Go up there and look at them. This is what many of my churches are like."

So I went and saw there also were people walking by outside the cage. I looked more closely and realized that the people in the cage thought they were *free* and thought the people outside were in *captivity!* They were deceived into thinking that captivity was freedom!

Preaching deliverance to captives is boldly speaking the truth in love and breaking the bondage of deception. That takes strength and anointing. The Church needs this kind of preaching, because so many are captives of sickness, captives of the flesh, captives of soulish theology, captives of the past, captives of bitterness, and so forth. Many are deceived and ignorant of the enemy's devices. The anointing blasts through those deceptions and brings the liberty of the truth. (John 8:32.)

To preach recovery of sight to the blind means both natural and spiritual blindness. Jesus opened blind physical eyes and blind spiritual eyes. Your physical eyes are valuable, but the eyes of the spirit are more important. In this day of great spiritual activity, if you have no discernment and cannot operate in the realm of the Spirit, you will be bound. Christians need to operate individually as well as corporately in the realm of the Holy Spirit.

To set at liberty them that are bruised requires tremendous strength and anointing. The Greek word translated as *bruised* does not mean a little black-and-blue mark you might get from bumping into something. According to *Strong's Exhaustive Concordance,* the Greek word *thrauo* means "crushed, shattered to minute pieces." People crushed by the enemy really need help from anointed ministers of God to receive healing and deliverance. The anointing will help put their lives back together according to the Word and teach them to stand against the devil.

What is *preaching the acceptable year of the Lord?* It is preaching the timings and seasons of God. We need to be aware of what God is doing in the earth and flow with Him as the anointings change. Right now, the season is changing. We are seeing God working in a different way from what we have become accustomed to.

We have been in a teaching season, but now we are moving into a preaching season. The teacher lays out points — one, two, three — but the preacher comes in with boldness and goes *kaboom.* The preacher must know how to flow in the anointing or he is a big loud "boom" that means nothing.

Preaching will be a part of God's weaponry against the devil in these last days.

The Power To Do Good

These are the things Jesus did as He ministered in the earth under the anointing of the Holy Spirit. He took bold action against the works of the enemy. He ministered in the power and authority of the Holy Spirit.

> How God anointed Jesus of Nazareth with the
> Holy Ghost and with power: who went about doing
> good, and healing all that were oppressed of the devil;
> for God was with him.
>
> Acts 10:38

Everywhere Jesus went, the anointing and power went with Him to heal, to deliver, to set free, and to destroy the works of the devil. **He came to destroy the works of the devil** (1 John 3:8). He was ministering under the anointing when He blessed the children and when He drove the moneychangers out of the temple. He was anointed when He fed the five thousand and when He cast out demons. He went about doing good for people and blasting the devil.

The anointing was for Jesus' ministry, but it was not for His day-to-day living. *He walked by faith in the everyday affairs of life.* He did not try to live in the anointing. His personal life was based on prayer and absolute obedience and submission to the Father.

> And when he had sent the multitudes away, he
> went up into a mountain apart to pray: and when the
> evening was come, he was there alone.
>
> Matthew 14:23

Jesus regularly went apart to pray and fellowship with the Father. That is when He got His "marching orders." There was no independent action in Jesus' life.

He prayed to the Father in faith, heard what the Father said, then went out and did what the Father said to do, and He did it under the anointing of the Holy Spirit. Jesus said:

> For I have not spoken of myself; but of the Father
> which sent me, he gave me a commandment, what I
> should say, and what I should speak.

> And I know that his commandment is life
> everlasting: whatsoever I speak therefore, even as the
> Father said unto me, so I speak.
>
> John 12:49,50

We can see from the life of Jesus that the anointing is for ministry to people. Also, the anointing is a mighty weapon against the enemy — a forward thrust to destroy the works of the devil, not just a defensive weapon to ward off attack. The anointing sets people free and defeats the enemy. The anointing breaks the yoke of bondage; it is the power to change things.

The anointing is for service and not for show. Jesus did not use the anointing to become a superstar; He ministered to the needs of the people. He did not use the anointing for personal gain or His own private affairs. It was *for* the public and *before* the public.

The anointing was not the dominant factor in Jesus' life. The dominant factor was His relationship with the Father. The anointing is important, but it is not the most important thing in life — God is.

The anointing is for everyone in the Body of Christ. Ecclesiastes 9:8 says, **Let thy head lack no ointment,** or anointing. We need the anointing to do the will of God, because we cannot do it out of the flesh. We cannot meet the needs of other people in our own strength and ability. It must be by the anointing of the Holy Spirit. **Not by might, nor by power, but by my spirit, saith the Lord of hosts** (Zech. 4:6).

Lucifer: the Anointed Cherub

There was a day when the devil was good. He was in heaven, and he was mightily anointed by God, but he made a wrong choice.

Thou hast been in Eden the garden of God; every precious stone was thy covering, the sardis, topaz, and the diamond, the beryl, the onyx, and the jasper, the sapphire, the emerald, and the carbuncle, and gold: the workmanship of they tabrets and of thy pipes was prepared in thee in the day that thou wast created.

Thou art the anointed cherub that covereth; and I have set thee so: thou wast upon the holy mountain of God; thou hast walked up and down in the midst of the stones of fire.

Thou wast perfect in thy ways from the day that thou wast created, till iniquity was found in thee.

By the multitude of thy merchandise they have filled the midst of thee with violence, and thou hast sinned: therefore I will cast thee as profane out of the mountain of God: and I will destroy thee, O covering cherub, from the midst of the stones of fire.

Thine heart was lifted up because of thy beauty, thou hast corrupted thy wisdom by reason of thy brightness: I will cast thee to the ground, I will lay thee before kings, that they may behold thee.

Thou hast defiled thy sanctuaries by the multitude of thine iniquities; by the iniquity of thy traffick; therefore will I bring forth a fire from the midst of thee, it shall devour thee, and I will bring thee to ashes upon the earth in the sight of all them that behold thee.

Ezekiel 28:13-18

Lucifer was the anointed cherub that covered. God created him perfect and set him upon His holy mountain. He had great wisdom and was right next to God. His beauty was beyond description, with *every* precious stone as his covering. His beauty was not just for the eyes but also for the ears, because he was in charge of the music of heaven. The musical instruments — tabrets and pipes — were within him.

Coveting the Glory

Lucifer had it made. He was under the anointing. He still understands the anointing. *He knows what kind of power is in the anointing. And he hates anyone who has the anointing, because he lost it.* His heart was lifted up in pride because of his beauty and his position. Pride covets the glory that belongs only to God. God will not share His glory with anyone. Then the pride in Lucifer opened the door to self-will and rebellion.

> How art thou fallen from heaven, O Lucifer, son of the morning! how art thou cut down to the ground, which didst weaken the nations!
>
> For thou hast said in thine heart, *I will* ascend into heaven, *I will* exalt my throne above the stars of God: *I will* sit also upon the mount of the congregation, in the sides of the north:
>
> *I will* ascend above the heights of the clouds; *I will* be like the most High.
>
> Yet thou shalt be brought down to hell, to the sides of the pit.
>
> They that see thee shall narrowly look upon thee, and consider thee, saying, Is this the man that made the earth to tremble, that did shake kingdoms;
>
> That made the world as a wilderness, and destroyed the cities thereof; that opened not the house of his prisoners?
>
> Isaiah 14:12-17

Notice all the "I wills" in those verses. Pride swelled in Lucifer's heart. He wanted the glory, and he decided to exalt himself and be like God. That decision was self-will. He put himself and what he wanted above God's will and entered into rebellion and treason. He came against the authority of God, and when you touch authority, you touch God Himself, because He is authority. Of course, God could not allow Lucifer to do what he planned, so there was war in heaven.

> And there was war in heaven: Michael and his angels fought against the dragon; and the dragon fought and his angels,
>
> And prevailed not; neither was their place found any more in heaven.
>
> And the great dragon was cast out, that old serpent, called the Devil, and Satan, which deceiveth the whole world: he was cast out into the earth, and his angels were cast out with him.
>
> Revelation 12:7-9

God did not call a committee meeting to mediate the dispute and decide which of them would be number one. No, there was war, and the devil was cast out of heaven.

But notice that the anointing is convincing. With what God had given him, Lucifer convinced a great multitude of angels that he was right to exalt himself. He convinced them that he would succeed in his plan, and their agreement cost them a place in heaven as well.

Can you imagine what God went through? Here was one of His prized creations coming against Him — a created being trying to make himself equal to the Creator! Lucifer used the power and anointing that God gave him to convince those about him in the angelic

47

realm that he was right. That was a real public relations campaign! They were so thoroughly convinced that they fought for Lucifer against Michael and the angels who stayed loyal to God.

Lucifer and his crowd lost that day: they lost their positions; they lost their anointings; they lost it all. They hate God and everyone who serves Him. So if you have made Jesus Lord of your life, welcome to boot camp. You are in the army of God. You can expect the enemy to come against you. He will do everything in his power to stop you from living for God. But Jesus provided the victory for us! We just have to learn how to war a good warfare.

4

Why the Mighty Heroes Have Fallen

In the Eighties, mighty heros of the faith fell flat on their faces. Thousands of people backslid because of the shock and disappointment. Of course, Christians should not lean on man, or look to other men. The fact is, however, that people should be able to trust spiritual leaders. These men have a responsibility to the Lord and their followers.

I sought the Lord as to why preachers fall. The answer He gave me is in this chapter. The same reason why men of God fall was true in Bible days.

Joseph and Samson were men of God with mighty anointings. Both had profound effects on their generations. Both were used by God. Both faced the same temptation. Both had the same opportunity to fall. One fell, but one did not. Why? Take a closer look at them, and you will see that one had *two* sources of strength, and the other only had *one* source.

> Now Israel loved Joseph more than all his children, because he was the son of his old age: and he made him a coat of many colours.
>
> And when his brethren saw that their father loved him more than all his brethren, they hated him, and could not speak peaceably unto him.
>
> And Joseph dreamed a dream, and he told it his brethren: and they hated him yet the more.
>
> **Genesis 37:3-5**

49

Joseph was in a very interesting position. His earthly father gave him more favor than his eleven brothers, even though he was not the firstborn. His brothers really resented his special treatment, but when God also began to use him more than them, they went into murderous hatred. Instead of killing Joseph, however, they sold him as a slave to a caravan of Ishmaelites on their way to Egypt, where he was re-sold to Potiphar, Pharaoh's captain of the guard.

And the Lord was with Joseph, and he was a prosperous man; and he was in the house of his master the Egyptian.

And his master saw that the Lord was with him, and that the Lord made all that he did to prosper in his hand.

And Joseph found grace in his sight, and he served him: and he made him overseer over his house, and all that he had he put into his hand.

And it came to pass from the time that he had made him overseer in his house, and over all that he had, that the Lord blessed the Egyptian's house for Joseph's sake; and the blessing of the Lord was upon all that he had in the house, and in the field.

And he left all that he had in Joseph's hand; and he knew not ought he had, save the bread which he did eat. *And Joseph was a goodly person, and well favored.*

Genesis 39:2-6

God was with him, and everything Joseph tried prospered. The anointing of God was upon him. Also, he was goodlooking and had inner strength. In spite of his circumstances, his character was solid.

50

Think about his situation. His own brothers sold him into slavery. It would be easy for anyone in his position to have a real attitude problem, to wallow in self-pity and rage with resentment. But he did not yield to those things. He did the best he could for his master while never losing sight of the dream God had given him. God blessed him and his master, because Joseph made the best of a difficult situation.

> And it came to pass after these things, that his master's wife cast her eyes upon Joseph; and she said, Lie with me.
>
> But he refused, and said unto his master's wife, Behold, my master wotteth not (does not have to think about) what is with me in the house, and he hath committed all that he hath to my hand;
>
> There is none greater in this house than I; neither hath he kept back any thing from me but thee, because thou art his wife: how then can I do this great wickedness, and sin against God?
>
> And it came to pass, as she spake to Joseph day by day, that he hearkened not unto her, to lie by her, or to be with her.
>
> **Genesis 39:7-10**

This is a graphic demonstration of Joseph's inner strength. He said, "No!" immediately when his master's wife propositioned him. Day after day she kept trying to seduce him, and he kept refusing. He continued to stand on his godly principles.

A Lack of Discipline

Contrast Joseph's actions with Samson's:

> Then went Samson to Gaza, and saw there an harlot, and went in unto her.
>
> **Judges 16:1**

Notice that Samson exercised no resistance at all. He saw the prostitute and immediately went in unto her. There was no restraint at all. "I want her, and I want her *now.*" He did not know how to say, "No," to his soul or body. Discipline was missing from his life.

A few verses later, we see that still another woman had become the object of his desires:

> **And it came to pass afterward, that he loved a woman in the valley of Sorek, whose name was Delilah.**
>
> **And the lords of the Philistines came unto her, and said unto her, Entice him, and see wherein his great strength lieth, and by what means we may prevail against him, that we may bind him to afflict him: and we will give thee every one of us eleven hundred pieces of silver.**
>
> **Judges 16:4,5**

Samson had been terrorizing the Philistine oppressors. Under the anointing, he had single-handedly killed more than a thousand of them. He carried off the gates of Gaza while the men in the city were waiting in ambush to kill him. The only weakness they could find in Samson was his lack of self-control where women were concerned. No other weapon was effective against him.

Delilah readily accepted the proposition of the Philistine leaders and used all her wiles to get Samson to tell her the secret of his great strength.

Instead of immediately refusing to reveal the secret of his power, Samson played with Delilah, lying to her three times about how his strength could be neutralized. Each time the Philistines were waiting to pounce on him, and each time he jumped up and whipped them.

Samson must have been pretty dense not to have seen the pattern there. His lust for the woman blinded him to what basic common sense would have shown him. He did not *deal* with the issue; he *played* with it.

And it came to pass, when she pressed him daily with her words, and urged him, so that his soul was vexed unto death;

That he told her all his heart . . . .
Judges 16:16,17

So Samson, who had an anointing that could paralyze the enemy by the hundreds, fell right down in the lap of a nagging Delilah and lost everything. No one else in the recorded history of Israel was anointed with the incredible physical strength manifested through Samson, yet he lost it all through lust of the flesh.

And she made him sleep upon her knees; and she called for a man, and she caused him to shave off the seven locks of his head; and she began to afflict him, and his strength went from him.

And she said, The Philistines be upon thee, Samson. And he awoke out of his sleep, and said, I will go out as at other times before, and shake myself. And he wist not that the Lord was departed from him.
Judges 16:19,20

Everyone faces "Delilah" in life. "Delilah" is not always a woman and sex problems. She may be many things: money, power, posessions, and so forth; anything that causes you to turn away from God's will for you. "Delilah" is *lust*, a consuming desire for something not of God, or uncontrolled wants. It causes a short circuit in your spiritual life.

What Was the Difference?

Why was Joseph able to resist when Samson could not? The temptation was the same. What factor made the difference? Why do the anointed fall?

My grandparents were Assemblies of God ministers, and they told me story after story about how they used to travel and start churches in North and South Carolina.

One story in particular really "bugged" me. There was a minister with such a powerful anointing that all he had to do was raise his hand, and everyone in the prayer line would be slain in the Spirit at once. Many healings took place. Yet he ran off with one of the women in the church and divorced his wife. It really bothered me that something like that could happen.

I studied some of the great men and women of God, and what I saw troubled me. How could John Alexander Dowie build a great city and be one of the greatest apostles of healing and yet die an invalid, believing he was Elijah?

In 1908, the great Azusa Street Revival waned because of a combination of strife among the brethren and spiritualism.

In 1955, miracle revivalist A. A. Allen was arrested for drunken driving.

In 1960, William Branham, a great prophet of God, began to teach heresy.

In 1987 and 1988, two televangelists — Jim Bakker and Jimmy Swaggart — fell in moral scandals.

How could these things happen? Did they love God with all their hearts? I believe the answer is yes. Did God really call them to preach the Gospel? Again, I believe the answer is yes. Then what happened to them that allowed such sin and error to overtake their lives and ministries?

I cried out to the Lord and studied the people of the Bible, and I believe the Lord has shown me one of the reasons these things are possible.

The anointing is not meant for our practical, everyday living. Strength of character, the authority of the inner man — the human spirit — gives us the ability to resist temptation and do what is right every day. The anointing does not help you resist sin.

Joseph's inner man was strong. He did not waver when temptation came. Samson's soul and body overpowered his spirit, causing him to yield immediately when he saw the prostitute. *Joseph had a strong inner man and the anointing; Samson only had the anointing.* Without a strong spirit, the soul and body of man will run wild, bringing destruction.

The anointing is for public service, not private life. Many people try to live off the anointing and fail to allow their spirits to be strong and fervent. A person with a weak inner man will not be able to take authority over his soul or body, and when the anointing lifts and temptation comes, he will fall as Samson did.

I began to find out that the key is not how anointed you are; it is how *strong* you are in your inner man behind closed doors that counts. Do you really know God and have that close, intimate relationship with Him in private, or do you only know the anointing for public service? Are you a public success and a private failure?

It is easy to live the Christian life when those around you are living that way. But where life really counts — where God will judge you the most — is behind closed doors in the privacy of your home.

I know ministers who are like Dr. Jekyll and Mr. Hyde. They have two personalities instead of one. Behind the pulpit, they are loving, strong and bold, but at home they have no strength, no joy, and no love. When the anointing begins to lift, they get depressed and go through great turmoil.

A minister's wife came to me after a service when I preached on this subject and said, "When I married my husband, he was the same man in both worlds. In the public and in the home, he was the same man. But now he's two different people. When he comes home, he's always depressed and worn out. He doesn't want to do anything but sit there and stare into outer space. And he's doing things that aren't right, and I don't know what to do about it."

I said, "Play the tape of this sermon (one I had preached on this same subject) a lot around him. Encourage him to pray in tongues and pray with him. Pray fervently, and begin to help him redevelop his inner man and put the Word inside him. Also give him time to allow his physical body to regain its strength."

Many people say, "Well, I've prayed," but they do not pray the right way. When they get behind closed doors, they pray weak, quiet prayers without authority. You have to stay in the Word and pray with authority to build your inner man. If you are going to be like Joseph instead of Samson, that is what you are going to have to do. It is not a one-shot deal; it is an everyday procedure. You have to build your inner man and keep your spirit strong.

When I first began in the ministry, I used to say, "If I could live behind the pulpit — if I could sleep, eat and do everything here — I'd have the most wonderful life."

I said that because when I left the pulpit and left the anointing, tremendous opposition would begin to come against me. I did not like it out from under the anointing.

Finally God said to me, "Why can't you have Me in the hotel room as strong as you have Me in the pulpit?"

I said, "Well, You know, why not?"

That is when He began to teach me, "You have to build your inner man. Your spirit must be strengthened."

I believe your spirit should be stronger than your anointing. Then there will be more joy in your ministry or work, and your life will not be a constant roller coaster ride. All that up-and-down business causes confusion in your life.

How To Build the Human Spirit

> Blessed is the man that endureth temptation: for when he is tried, he shall receive the crown of life, which the Lord hath promised to them that love him.
>
> Let no man say when he is tempted, I am tempted of God: for God cannot be tempted with evil, neither tempteth he any man:
>
> But every man is tempted, when he is drawn away of his own lust, and enticed. ˙
>
> Then when lust hath conceived, it bringeth forth sin: and sin, when it is finished, bringeth forth death.
> James 1:12-15

The Word does not say, "Blessed is the man who avoids testing, or does not deal with temptation, or runs from trials." It says, **Blessed is the man that endureth temptation.** The *New American Standard Bible* translates it as **Blessed is a man who perseveres under trial.** Enduring and persevering speak to us about going through the test or trial and coming out on the other side victorious.

The Lord does not want us to run from what we have to deal with, because whatever we run from will one day own us. Some people want to go over the mountain. Some want to go under it. Others want to go around it, but God has called us to go *through* it. What makes you strong is drilling through something.

Too many people today do not want to go through anything. They will not even go through God's boot camp. They are always looking for the easy way out, which is why they cannot overcome temptation. Their souls and bodies are so out from under authority that their spirits are never able to take charge of anything.

Then when temptation comes, they fall like Samson, because they do not have what is necessary to resist.

If you want to be like Joseph and not like Samson, there are certain principles you need to live by. You need to build these principles on the inside and keep them established, so you can live every day the way God wants you to live. They will bring you into stability and get you off the roller coaster, where one minute you are ready to take on the whole world and the next minute, you can hardly get up and breathe.

The Apostle Paul prayed that Jesus **would grant you, according to the riches of his glory, to be strengthened with might by his Spirit in the inner man** (Eph. 3:16). Paul knew the value of having a strong inner man. The strength of his spirit helped him go through one trial after another and come out victorious and unwavering.

You build up the human spirit by 1) staying in the Word, 2) praying fervently, 3) surrendering everything to God, and 4) keeping the correct associations.

Stay in the Word

Your physical body needs food regularly to maintain its strength and so does your spirit. The inner man feeds on the Word of God. Dr. Kenneth E. Hagin often says that too many Christians feed their bodies three square meals a day but only give their spirits one cold snack a week. Your spirit needs a daily diet of the Word to grow strong and bear fruit.

But he that received seed into the good ground is he that heareth the word, and understandeth it;

which also beareth fruit, and bringeth forth, some an hundredfold, some sixty, and some thirty.

Matthew 12:23

But the fruit of the Spirit is love, joy, peace, longsuffering, gentleness, goodness, faith,

Meekness, temperance: against such there is no law.

And they that are Christ's have crucified the flesh with the affections and lusts.

If we live in the Spirit, let us also walk in the Spirit.

Galatians 5:22-25

Consistently sowing the Word into your inner man will make your spirit stronger. The stronger your inner man becomes, the more fruit you will see in your life. Walking in the Spirit means that you have crucified the flesh — taken full authority over your soul and body — so that every part of your being is in submission to Christ and bearing fruit is a way of life, not an occasional thing. The proper *alignment* of spirit, soul, and body is of great importance for building a strong inner man.

Staying in the Word also brings freedom from bondage.

Then said Jesus to those Jews which believed on him, If ye continue in my word, then are ye my disciples indeed;

And ye shall know the truth, and the truth shall make you free.

John 8:31,32

When God commissioned Joshua to lead the children of Israel into the Promised Land, He said:

> **This book of the law shall not depart out of thy
> mouth; but thou shalt meditate therein day and night,
> that thou mayest observe to do according to all that
> is written therein: for then thou shalt make thy way
> prosperous, and then thou shalt have good success.**
> **Joshua 1:8**

These scriptures show that staying in the Word
builds the inner man to bear good fruit and walk in
freedom, prosperity and success. Without the Word,
the inner man will grow weaker and weaker, yielding
a fruitless life of bondage, poverty and failure. The
choice is yours.

Pray Fervently

James 5:16 says, **The effectual fervent prayer of a
righteous man availeth much.** It is how fervent you are
in your prayer life and Bible study that will determine
how strong you will be with God.

What is *fervent* prayer? It is intense and involved.
It means that your spirit, soul and body are all involved.
When you pray, is your mind with you, or is it in
another world? Is your body with you, or is it wanting
to lie down instead of pray? If your soul and body are
split like that, you cannot pray fervently. Your house
is divided against itself.

> **And if a house be divided against itself, that
> house cannot stand.**
> **Mark 3:25**

You cannot pray with boldness, intensity and
authority until you get your mind, emotions and body
under the control of the spirit, so you can stay in there.
You need to press into the Kingdom of God, and you

do that by keeping yourself together. Do not let yourself be concerned over other things during prayer.

Surrender Everything to God

I beseech you therefore, brethren, by the mercies of God, that ye present your bodies a living sacrifice, holy, acceptable unto God, which is your reasonable service.

And be not conformed to this world: but be ye transformed by the renewing of your mind, that ye may prove what is that good, and acceptable, and perfect, will of God.

Romans 12:1,2

Verily, verily, I say unto you, Except a corn of wheat fall into the ground and die, it abideth alone: but if it die, it bringeth forth much fruit.

John 12:24

When I went through what I call my six years of training in my bedroom Bible school, I said, "God, is there anything left You're going to let me keep? What else do you want, Lord? I've given You everything."

The Lord said, "I want everything you are."

There is a two-fold dying involved here: There is a death in just giving over to the Lord, and there is a death of getting everything right. The second one is worse than the first.

Everything you hold to, God will remove. I would hold to something, and the next afternoon it would leave.

The Lord said, "You will get to the place where it is just Me and you. And you will let Me direct the occurrences of your life and the righteousness of your life."

"But, Lord, it's hard, and it hurts."

He said, "Didn't you die?"

"But, Lord, I'm still living."

"That's why I'm still clipping," He said.

Jesus said in John 15:1,2 (NAS):

> "I am the true vine, and My Father is the vinedresser.
>
> "Every branch in Me that does not bear fruit, He takes away; and every branch that bears fruit, He prunes it, that it may bear more fruit."

Your inner man gets stronger as you surrender everything to God and allow Him to prune away the things that sap your strength. Jesus is the Vine, and the more you surrender to Him and abide in Him, the more of His strength flows into you. Unsurrendered areas in your life block the flow of His power and make you unfruitful.

> "Abide in Me, and I in you. As a branch cannot bear fruit of itself, unless it abides in the vine, so neither can you, unless you abide in Me.
>
> "I am the vine, you are the branches; he who abides in Me, and I in him, he bears much fruit; for apart from Me you can do nothing.
>
> "If anyone does not abide in Me, he is thrown away as a branch, and dries up; and they gather them, and cast them into the fire, and they are burned.
>
> "If you abide in Me, and My words abide in you, ask whatever you wish, and it shall be done for you.

> "By this is My Father glorified, that you bear
> much fruit, and so prove to be My disciples."
> John 15:4-8 NAS

If you are acting independently of God in any area of your life, you are not abiding in the Vine in that area. Even if it appears to be a good work or a righteous thing, if it is independent of God and unsurrendered to Him, it is of no value. It is unfruitful and needs to be pruned.

As you surrender to God in spirit, soul and body, your inner man will be strengthened with might, so you can immediately say, "No!" when temptation comes and keep on saying it, just like Joseph.

The Apostle Paul said nothing was of any value compared with knowing Jesus as Lord.

> But what things were gain to me, those I counted loss for Christ.
>
> Yea, doubtless, and I count all things but loss for the excellency of the knowledge of Christ Jesus my Lord: for whom I have suffered the loss of all things, and do count them but dung, that I may win Christ,
>
> And be found in him, not having mine own righteousness, which is of the law, but that which is through the faith of Christ, the righteousness which is of God by faith:
>
> That I may know him, and the power of his resurrection, and the fellowship of his sufferings, being made conformable unto his death;
>
> If by any means I might attain unto the resurrection of the dead.
> Philippians 3:7-11

God cannot resurrect something that is not dead. Surrender everything to Him and abide in Him. Then He can resurrect those areas in the right way, and if He does not resurrect some things, you do not need them. Just let them go and go on with God.

Associate With Godly People

The people around you can have a strong effect on your inner man. Surround yourself with Godly men and women, people who are submitted to God. You need to be with those of like, or stronger, spirits, not with those whose souls or bodies are in control.

If you spend all your time with weak, carnal Christians, you may find yourself getting weaker and weaker. I am not telling you to avoid weak Christians, but make sure you have quality time with people who will help you grow spiritually.

The power to overcome temptation is not found in the anointing. It is found in the building up and development of the human spirit. It is found in keeping the soul and body in line with the spirit. Discouragement will not win over you when you are strong in your inner man. Doubts and fears will not manipulate you and control your life when you are strong in the spirit. You will just laugh at them.

You can be like Smith Wigglesworth, who said, "I'm a thousand times bigger on the inside than I am on the outside!"

5

How To Stir Up the Gifts of God

> Now there are varieties of gifts, but the same Spirit.
>
> And there are varieties of ministries, and the same Lord.
>
> And there are varieties of effects, but the same God who works all things in all persons.
>
> But to each one is given the manifestation of the Spirit for the common good.
>
> 1 Corinthians 12:4-7 NAS

If you are a believer, you have a gift of God within you. Every believer does. The gift might not be a pulpit ministry, or even a ministry of helps, but you have a gift that God has placed in you. Many gifts of God are dormant because people do not recognize them or do not know how to get them to flow through their lives. Christians need to learn to enjoy the gifts and to take the responsibility of flowing with them.

> Wherefore I put thee in remembrance that thou stir up the gift of God, which is in thee by the putting on of my hands.
>
> 2 Timothy 1:6

The Apostle Paul was writing here to his young pastor friend, Timothy, and reminding him to **stir up the gift of God**. *The New International Version* says **to fan into flame the gift of God**. We have to do something with the gift or gifts of God. They do not come forth automatically.

Paul was reminding Timothy about some of the things he had written in his first letter.

These things command and teach.

Let no man despise thy youth; but be thou an example of the believers, in word, in conversation, in charity, in spirit, in faith, in purity.

Till I come, give attendance to reading, to exhortation, to doctrine.

Neglect not the gift that is in thee, which was given thee by prophecy, with the laying on of the hands of the presbytery.

Meditate upon these things; give thyself wholly to them; that thy profiting may appear to all.

Take heed unto thyself, and unto the doctrine; continue in them: for in doing this thou shalt both save thyself, and them that hear thee.

1 Timothy 4:11-16

Paul's words are good advice for any minister, but particularly for a young minister. Notice that he said **command and teach** these things.

He did not say, "Present them, and if you like them, do something with them."

No, **command and teach** means: "You are an example. Make yourself do it whether you want to or not, then teach the people of the church, and command them to do it also."

It takes boldness and confidence in the Lord to command instead of suggest. Do not let anyone despise you or look down on you with contempt because of your physical age or your spiritual age. You can be twenty years old in the natural and spiritually be thirty-five. Be bold, and do not let your physical age hold you back.

You can be forty in the natural and a year old in the spirit. But do not let anyone look down on you for being a year old. Be bold in that year; be strong in it; be happy in it. There is nothing wrong with being a year old spiritually — unless you have been a Christian for many years. In that case, it is time to grow up. No matter what your age is, rise up and rejoice in the Lord. Be an example to others.

Neglect not the gift that is in thee (v. 14). Christians who say, "I don't have anything. God didn't give me anything," just do not know their gifts yet.

There is something in you that needs to come out. Do not look for it in your head, because it is not there. It is in your spirit man, the real you. God put something in your spirit, and you need to stir it up and cause it to come forth like a mighty river. You need to take action.

Do Not Hide the Gift

One of the parables of Jesus clearly deals with this matter:

> For the kingdom of heaven is as a man travelling into a far country, who called his own servants, and delivered unto them his goods.
>
> And unto one he gave five talents, to another two, and to another one; to *every man* according to his several ability; and straightway took his journey.
>
> Then he that had received the five talents went and traded with the same, and made them other five talents.

69

And likewise he that had received two, he also gained other two.

And he that had received one went and digged in the earth, and hid his lord's money.

After a long time the lord of those servants cometh, and reckoneth with them.

And so he that had received five talents came and brought other five talents, saying, Lord, thou deliveredst unto me five talents: behold, I have gained beside them five talents more.

His lord said unto him, Well done, thou good and faithful servant: thou hast been faithful over a few things, I will make thee ruler over many things: enter thou into the joy of thy lord.

He also that had received two talents came and said, Lord, thou deliveredst unto me two talents: behold, I have gained two other talents beside them.

His lord said unto him, Well done, good and faithful servant; thou hast been faithful over a few things, I will make thee ruler over many things: enter thou into the joy of thy lord.

Then when he which had received the one talent came and said, Lord, I knew thee that thou art an hard man, reaping where thou hast not sown, and gathering where thou hast not strawed:

And I was afraid, and went and hid thy talent in the earth: lo, there thou hast that is thine.

His lord answered and said unto him, Thou wicked and slothful servant, thou knewest that I reap where I sowed not, and gather where I have not strawed:

Thou oughtest therefore to have put my money to the exchangers, and then at my coming I should have received mine own with usury.

Take therefore the talent from him, and give it unto him which hath ten talents.

For unto every one that hath shall be given, and he shall have abundance: but from him that hath not shall be taken away even that which he hath.

And cast ye the unprofitable servant into outer darkness: there shall be weeping and gnashing of teeth.

Matthew 25:14-30

The talents in the parable were gifts of God, shown in the parable to be like money, to be invested and multiplied or wasted. Each man had one or more, according to his abilities. The men who exercised or used their gifts were rewarded with more, and that made their Lord joyful. They showed themselves worthy of more. The man who hid his gift and did not use it was called a lazy, unprofitable servant, and he lost what he did have.

Feed Your Spirit

So how do you get that gift unwrapped? How do you cause it to flow out with ease? Let me show you some things that have worked for me — things that have made a difference in my own life.

I used to listen to certain ministry tapes over and over. At first, the tapes taught me. I enjoyed them, and they built me up. I did not want to put them aside. But after a while, those tapes left me flat.

I thought, "Now what's wrong here? There's nothing wrong with that man or his message, so there must be something wrong with me."

God said, "You need something with more 'oomph' to it. You've learned all you can from that. Find something that feeds your spirit. Find something that stirs you up, that gets you excited, that gets you joyful. Find something like that."

That did not mean I did not like those first preachers anymore. I *still* love them and love to hear them. But now I had to find someone who had something additional to feed my spirit. I needed a change of diet.

Find people who feed you and feed your anointing and calling. Find people who will stretch your spiritual understanding and knowledge. If you want to walk in the power of God, you need to listen to preachers who have power. Stop associating with dead things. When you are no longer being fed what you need to do is move where there is spiritual food for you.

If you are trying to feed your inner man with weak or dead things, you will be wishy-washy and powerless. You will be afraid to deliver the word of the Lord. You will wonder if you are really hearing God. But if your spirit has been stirred up and fed, you will not wonder; you will *know* it is the word of the Lord. You will be able to stand up against all the forces of hell and say it is right. You will be as solid as the Rock of Gibraltar.

Associate, visit, and spend time with people who stir you up, people who can get you up and doing something. Be bold in the power of God. If you want to get results, get bold. If you want to stay weak, keep associating with dead preachers and dead churches.

Speak It Forth

The gifts of God respond to bold calls.

When you boldly say: "Gift of God that is within me, come forth; stir up like a river; spring up within me in Jesus' name," it will come.

But do not do it one time and wait. *Keep doing it* until the gift begins to come forth. Soon you will not be saying, "Come forth." You will be speaking in other tongues, and that gift will begin to operate.

I walk my bedroom floor and cause the gift that is within me to spring up. I cause the gift to move, because I call for it to come forth in Jesus' name.

I say, "Gift, you belong to me, and you will not leave this vessel, because you are mine. God, the Creator of heaven and earth, has given you unto me for the work of the Kingdom. And this day, I call you forth. I call you forth up out of me. Let the word of the Lord come forth. Let the gifts of God come forth."

And I pull at it. I pull inwardly, and I pull by my voice, by speaking it forth. As you speak and pull, your voice needs to have power behind it. You words cannot be skinny; they need to be fat and powerful. You can say all the right words, but "wimpy" words will not change you.

You need to learn to speak to yourself and make yourself obedient to God. (Eph. 5: 19.) You have to take control. Your mind is like a spoiled child that has to be corrected very often. Teach it to enjoy the Gospel. Teach it to enjoy praying in tongues.

When it is hard, make yourself get happy. Look in the mirror and make yourself smile. You have to cause yourself to rejoice when there is no rejoice in you. This is an example of how to pray when you do not feel like rejoicing:

Oh, my soul, why are you disquieted? Why are you disturbed within me? Rejoice! Rejoice! Blessed be the name of the Lord forever. Blessed is the name of the Lord. The Lord is good, and His mercy endures forever. His truth shall endure to every generation. No enemy can steal that.

I am a victor. I am more than a conqueror because Jesus has set me free. He set me on high because He loved me. There is nothing that I cannot overcome through Jesus Christ.

I believe in God, and I believe in His Son and His Holy Spirit. He is my friend and my Savior. I trust in Him. I lean on the everlasting arms. I seek His face continually. My soul does rejoice after the God of my salvation. I will not linger or wait; I will continue on the path that He has set before me.

Thank You, Lord Jesus. Let my soul rejoice. Let me jump for everlasting joy. Let my heart sing the new songs of glory. Let my ears hear the words of the Lord. Let my eyes see into the Spirit realm and let my hands feel the power of the moving of the Spirit of the Living God. Let your praises be continually in my mouth. Thank You, Lord.

If you are going to be part of God's invading force, you should start doing what God tells you to do with wisdom.

He says, "Stir up the gifts; walk in the power."

You have to do something: You have to walk by faith. For the first few months of your life in the Spirit, you will not have goose bumps every morning when you wake up. You will not wake up with the Word of the Lord in your mouth every morning.

You may wake up with the words of failure surrounding you. The devil will try to fill you with doubt and depression. He will try to make you doubt what God has told you to do. When the devil starts that business, jump on him with both feet. Preach him a sermon on the gifts and callings of God, and make him understand who you are in Christ Jesus. Attack him! If you sit there and listen to him long enough you will die; but, if you attack, you will drive him out of your life.

Do Not Be Ashamed of Your Gift

Do not be ashamed of what God is doing in your life. Do not be ashamed of what God has called you to do.

When God told me to go into the nations of the earth and preach the Gospel, I did not know how. I had no money; I had no contacts but Him. So I kept walking the floors and calling forth the gift:

"I'm called, and I shall be successful. I will not go any other way but the way that God desires for me to go. No matter what comes,

I shall overcome. Why? Because the Greater One lives within me. I heed His voice.

"No one shall cause me to deviate from the path that God has called me to walk. No one shall cause me to be ashamed, because I glory in Christ, and I obey His voice. I rejoice in the Lord, my God, and I shall succeed in Jesus' name."

If you will authoritatively speak things like that every morning and every lunchtime and every evening, soon it will happen. God likes people who are bold in His service. I am not ashamed to say that I am called to the fivefold ministry. I am glad I am what I am. Also, I am glad I am not you, and *you* should be glad you are not me. Do not try to be me — be yourself.

If you are a psalmist, make music.

If you are an usher, usher.

If you are a businessman, get down to business and do it joyfully. Do not let the devil try to get you to stop doing business. As soon as you know you are anointed to do business, the devil will come along and try to tell you that you are a preacher. Watch out!

Not everyone is called to the fivefold ministry. Trying to call yourself to an office will cause you as much trouble as not answering a call God has for you. *Do what God has called you to do.* Stir up that business gift.

You need to protect your gift, because there are hindrances that will come to you. There are spirits of the enemy who will come to hinder you. They will try to destroy the operation of your gift or cause it to be laid aside. Watch your gift as though it is a little baby. It is real small, and you have to carry it. You have to care for it and guard it.

You need to say, "Lord, where do You want me to go so I can let my baby gift grow a little? What book do You want me to read?"

Do not read everything on the shelf. Use some common sense. Ask the Lord what you need to read in order to change and grow. You do not need to be weird to be spiritual. God does not bless weirdness. He does not bless stupidity and laziness, either. When that baby gift is born, you have to take care of it, or you will be a bad parent, a bad steward. If you do not, you may not get any more gifts. God does not give more to people who do not do anything with what they already have.

Do you know why some of the great spiritual leaders keep getting greater? Because they show themselves worthy of more. God watches you to see what you do with His gift.

When the new gift comes, God does not give it to you on a silver platter. He puts it in you, but you need to call it forth and give birth to it. The greater it is, the more battles you will go through. As you call your gift forth, it will begin to flow. Allow it to flow. Keep it flowing. Exercise it.

When I minister, I give myself over to the Holy Spirit. I set myself aside so He can manifest through me, and the gift can flow freely.

Commit yourself to "let go and let God." Feed your spirit man, boldly speak forth your gift, protect your gift, keep it flowing, and never be ashamed of what God has called and equipped you to do.

6
How To Be Fervent

This man was instructed in the way of the Lord; and being *fervent* in the spirit, he spake and taught diligently the things of the Lord....

Acts 18:25

Not slothful in business; *fervent* in spirit; serving the Lord.

Romans 12:11

Confess your faults one to another, and pray one for another, that ye may be healed. The effectual *fervent* prayer of a righteous man availeth much.

James 5:16

The key word in these three verses is *fervent*, which speaks of *authoritative strength*. Notice that this authoritative strength is not in the flesh, but in the spirit.

Most people who read James 5:16 think, "Oh, a righteous man's prayer does a lot of work."

But the little word *fervent* can make as much difference to your prayers being answered as understanding righteousness.

As a traveling minister, I often have people walk up to me and say something like this:

"I've been praying three hours a day for a month. I've been praying every way, every confession I know, and it doesn't seem to be working."

If there is a problem in our prayer lives, it is *not* God's fault. The problem has to be in us, and we need to diagnose it and find a solution. We need to find out what we are doing wrong and correct it.

Some of the people who tell me they have been praying for hours and have not gotten an answer are lying. They really have not been praying that long. They are trying to be superspiritual to impress someone, instead of just being themselves. Anyone with a little discernment will see through a facade, and honesty will make a better impression.

Some of the people who are not getting anywhere in prayer are just plain ignorant. They do not know what the Bible says about prayer, so they do their own thing, but God is not in it.

However, some of the people are not lying, ignorant, or flaky. They *have* been seeking God. They *have* been praying and not getting an answer, and they want to know why. They have been doing everything they know to do but have not gotten the breakthrough, the answer they need from heaven.

A House Divided

I began to ask, "God, why aren't these people getting an answer?"

It bothered me because I was raised in a home where as soon as we went to God He said, "What?" And we quickly got an answer. So when I entered the world of ministry and began hearing more and more about people who had trouble getting hold of God, I thought, "What's the problem?"

As I prayed about it, the Lord took me to James 5:16 and said, "The effectual *fervent* prayer of a righteous man availeth much."

He made the word *fervent* stand out to me. Then he took me to Matthew 12:25:

> **And Jesus knew their thoughts, and said unto them, Every kingdom divided against itself is brought to desolation; and every city or house divided against itself shall not stand.**

Individually, you are a kingdom or a house, and you have three distinct parts: You are a spirit; you have a soul; and you live in a body.

The spirit is the *real* you, and the soul and body are tools for you to use to function in the earth. When your physical body dies, it is discarded and it will be replaced by a resurrection body when Jesus returns. But your soul — your mind, will and emotions — will go with your spirit man when you go to heaven. They are attached. You have to deal with the soul *here* as well as *there*.

First Peter 1:13 says to gird your mind for action — in other words, bring your soul under control so you will be ready for action. You are not a mind; you *have* a mind. There is a big difference.

God's proper order is for the body to be in submission to the soul, for the soul to be in submission to the spirit, and for the whole man — spirit, soul and body — to be in submission to Him. Sadly, far too many Christians are out of order. They are walking around with uncontrolled souls or bodies that are dictating to or blocking their spirits. A weak inner man cannot control an untamed soul. That was Samson's problem. He could not say, "No," to his soul or body.

If your three parts are divided, you will fall. When you pray, if you are trying to pray, and your body wants to sleep, you are divided, and you are not fervent.

To be fervent means to have your spirit, your soul and your body go together as one into that arena of prayer and worship.

There is a level of intensity that can only be reached when your three parts are united and functioning as one. James 5:16 could be paraphrased as "the intense prayer of a rightous man is very effective."

Most of us pray divided. Our bodies want to sleep or eat or go do something else. Our minds are jumping from one thing to another. If you allow your body and mind to do these things while you are in prayer, you are divided and not fervent. You have to get your soul and body under the leadership of your spirit to be fervent and avail much.

Sometimes when you start praying, your mind will tell you everything you have not done, and it might get so strong that you will quit praying and go do it. When I began to train my mind to stay with me in prayer, I would write down what it would tell me that I had not done yet. Pretty soon I would have a major list of things to do.

But finally I said, "No, mind, you're going to obey me."

You have to make your head obey you. Sometimes you have to speak to your head and say, "Head, if you don't agree with me — if you keep fighting me — I am going to pray an extra fifteen minutes in other tongues."

I learned how to pray as a child by watching my mother and grandmother pray. When they hit a certain realm in the Spirit, the power of God would fall in the room. Many people never get out into that realm of the Spirit, or they only get there when they are in trouble and need some money. God wants us to *live* in that realm. That is what makes the Christian life exciting.

It Takes a Choice

You will never feel like praying fervently. It is a choice you have to make and keep making. Begin making that choice, and God will meet you there. Use your willpower to grab your soul and body and make them join your spirit in prayer.

Acts 18:25 refers to a minister who was fervent in spirit. The means he disciplined himself, and when he went out to preach, his whole being preached with him. That is what I try to do when I preach.

My head is not thinking, "I need to go home and take care of that," and my body is not saying, "I wish I could sleep."

No, when I get in the pulpit, all three parts — spirit, soul and body — are there to preach and preach fervently. When I preach like that, the power flows and the church gets a full meal. Too many Christians are only getting half a meal on Sunday because their pastors are not all together in the pulpit. Some do not even get half a meal, just a cold snack or half a glass of milk.

Romans 12:11 says we should be fervent in spirit. That means to live fervently. God wants us to pray fervently, preach fervently, and live fervently. When you say something, you should believe it and stand on it — spirit, soul and body. If you will live like that, you will not be so easily deceived or scared. There is strength when you are all together.

Some Christians live in fear all the time. As soon as they get away from the presence of strong Christians, their heads pull them back into the arena of fear and away from faith. Not being together leaves them weak and vulnerable to attack from spirits of fear.

People who are not together are confused, because they do not know what they are going to do next. They have three directions: They can go the body way, the head way, or the spirit way. They sit there in the flesh, get worried and frustrated, and usually end up doing nothing.

Many people live like that. That is why their decisions never stick. When they make a decision, about three minutes later their heads talk them out of it, or their bodies do not want to do it, so they forget about it. They are not fervent, and their divided houses will fall. You can be fervent without any problem when you know you are *standing on truth*.

> **And he answering said, Thou shalt love the Lord thy God with all thy heart, and with all thy soul, and with all thy strength, and with all thy mind; and thy neighbor as thyself.**
>
> **Luke 10:27**

God expects us to love Him with all of our being, holding nothing back. He expects us to approach Him in prayer the same way, with heart and soul and strength and mind united.

Your spirit knows that your mind and body have to be in agreement with it to have an effectual prayer. Your spirit will try to pull everything together. But if your flesh outweighs it, if the flesh can pull harder, your spirit will wear itself out, and your prayer will not avail much.

This is why people often waste time when they try to pray. The whole time they are praying, they cannot wait to get through and do something else. They are going through the motions. They are not really praying — just on their way through something to something else. They are praying as a formula instead of as a productive part of their lives.

If you are just praying because it is the thing to do, it stinks. God does not want your formula. He wants *you*. He wants you to humble your whole being before Him and pray fervently. He wants you to live like that and work like that. Fervency should be your lifestyle.

If you are going to be a Christian, be one. Forget about being religious. Religion is having a form of godliness but denying the power thereof. Religion is disgusting to God. He wants a relationship with you, not a bunch of religious barriers and jargon. The Bible says to be either hot or cold, right or wrong, in or out, but not lukewarm. Either you are with God or you are not.

Far too many Christians are religious. They do just enough Christianity mixed with just enough flesh to stay miserable. And that is no way to live. That is being lukewarm. (Rev. 3:15,16.)

Fervent Christians have joy and all the other fruit of the Spirit. It is fun to be fervent, because you are totally involved. You are in it all the way.

Fervent Christians are the ones who are going to last in the difficult days ahead. They are the ones who will be overcomers. The devil comes to kill, to steal and to destroy, and if he can divide you, he has you. A house divided will fall quickly in difficult times.

Fervent Prayers Get Answered

You can be sitting there praying in tongues, and your body will say, "I don't want to pray in tongues anymore. I want to pray in English."

Soon your flesh is dominating your spiritual activities, instead of your spirit dominating your flesh. No wonder you cannot get results. You can wear yourself out going three hours a day trying to find God.

Do not say, "Well, I'm trying to be a good Christian."

Stop trying and do it!

There is no way you can pray fervently and not get God to answer. It is like when children are playing, and they say, "Mom." The mother knows it is no big deal and just goes on with what she is doing. Then it comes: "MOM!" And she drops everything and immediately responds. What was the difference? The second call was fervent. All three parts were calling out at the same time, and Mom knew it.

That is how we need to talk to God. All three parts need to go, "GOD!" It is not desperation, it is intensity. I believe if you pray like that, God will hit you with an answer within an hour or two, sometimes sooner. I believe if you learn to be fervent and consistent, you can say, "God!" and He will say, "What?"

God does not talk to your head. He talks to your spirit — the real you. So remember, God is going to talk to your belly, because that is where the spirit man sits. Your head might find out about it a few seconds later, but God is going to speak to the real you first.

Fervent in Church

You need to be fervent everytime you go to church if you want God's best. If you let your flesh rule, you will not have much fun in church. One time your head will want to be intellectual, and you will sit there criticizing the sermon. Another day your body will get mad at the wooden pews and distract you. Your head can be miles away, and you can still sit there and smile.

You will say, "Well, I never get fed at that church."

You never came to that church.

Your spirit, soul and body need to be united when you are at church, not going three different directions. You will not be able to recognize what the Holy Spirit is doing in a service if you are not all together. A glory cloud could roll in and fill the auditorium, and you would not know it, if your head was off thinking about the job, or your body was worrying about the lines at the cafeteria that afternoon.

Make your body walk through the church door. Make your head come with your spirit through that door. Come in there together. If a spirit of heaviness is trying to weigh you down, get fervent in praise and worship, and drive that spirit far from you.

Look at what happened when the worshipers came together as one during the days of King Solomon:

> It came even to pass, as the trumpeters and singers were as one, to make one sound to be heard in praising and thanking the Lord; and when they lifted up their voice with the trumpets and cymbals and instruments of musick, and praised the Lord, saying, For he is good; for his mercy endureth for ever: that then the house was filled with a cloud, even the house of the Lord;
>
> So that the priests could not stand to minister by reason of the cloud: for the glory of the Lord had filled the house of God.
>
> **2 Chronicles 5:13,14**

I believe the same thing can happen in any church of the Living God if the people will come together and fervently praise and worship. I believe God's heart is yearning to manifest His presence in a greater way in His Church.

But before you can get in unity with everyone else, you have to get your own being in unity.

Then you need to learn how to hook up with the other people. Both of them are decisions you have to make every time. You will not do either one automatically. You have to choose to be in unity. When you set your will to do that, you will learn to flow with what God is doing in the services.

Get fervent in prayer. Get fervent in church. Get fervent in every area of your life, and you will find that God will meet you in new and exciting ways. Learn to jump in there and flow with Him, because new things are on the way.

7

The Lord Is a Warrior

Some people do not like to discuss the devil, but I believe we need to learn about our enemy, so we are able to wage a better war and understand his strategies. *Never forget that we are in a war.* Many people seem to believe that the supernatural realm is imaginary, that somehow it is not real. What an incredible deception! The world of the spirit is *more real* than the natural realm.

Satan and his hierarchies are not dumb. They know what they are doing. They know human nature and plan their strategies and attacks accordingly. They study our weaknesses and use them against us. Their goal is destruction and death.

My parents taught me about one of the devil's greatest attacks, particularly against young ministers.

They said, "Now, Roberts, listen...listen.

"Listen to us," they said, "the devil doesn't really mind that you love God as a young man. He'll fight you a little, but he won't fight you too much now. He'll wait until you get to be well-known, when a lot of people will trust your ministry. He has planned his strategy and found any weaknesses in your flesh that have not been dealt with. Then when it will hurt the most, he'll hit you at a weak moment and try to knock you out. Most of the time he's very successful."

When the devil knocks out a big ministry, he knocks out thousands of people who trusted that ministry. The repercussions ripple throughout the Body of Christ. So we all need to be aware of the devil's devices.

There are three major "killer weapons of the devil" that have been knocking out ministries for generations. If you are a young minister, watching out for these things could save your ministry and possibly your life.

Killer No. 1: Pride

Pride caused Satan's fall from heaven and has destroyed many ministries. It is the biggest ditch found in the supernatural realm. People fall into it by the thousands.

Pride is a secret killer. Very subtly, it sets up its home inside you — in your heart. It begins to feed you thoughts that at first you may forget or throw out. But it will keep feeding them to you. Yes, pride has a voice, and it will talk to you where no one else can hear it. What pride says will *seem* to be true, but it is a trap. Pride always speaks when you are at the point of needing encouragement, when you need someone to say that you are on the right track.

Pride will come in and say, "Yes, you're doing a wonderful job. Look at what happens when people come to your meetings. Look at what you have accomplished for God."

If you accept those thoughts, the big "I" will start growing in you, and then the "I wills" will move you from pride to self-will and rebellion, leaving you primed for a big fall. When you walk in humility, God will promote you. When you step over into pride, God will demote you.

Saul is a good example. When he was humble, God anointed him to be the first king over Israel, but he lost it all because he stepped over into pride and disobedience. He did not remain little in his own eyes.

Look at what pride does in your life:

First, *pride brings strife.* Proverbs 13:10 says, **Only by pride cometh contention: but with the well advised is wisdom.**

Second, *pride hardens the mind.*

> **But when his heart was lifted up, and his mind hardened in pride, he was deposed from his kingly throne, and they took his glory from him.**
> **Daniel 5:20**

As pride hardens your mind, you cannot think straight. It causes you to make decisions that bring failure. Pride makes you think you can do something when you are not really ready, then you fall when you try to do it. Pride also makes you think you can do things in your own strength without God.

Third, *pride produces spiritual decay.* (Hosea 7:9,10.) It keeps you from real progress. Pride stunts your spiritual growth, because it says you have arrived and no longer need to work for maturity. Remember this: with God there is no beginning, and there is no end, so there will always be a progression.

There will never be a day of saying, "I've got it all together."

Fourth, *pride insulates you from godly counsel.* (Prov. 13:10.) Pride will surround itself with flatterers and "yes men," people who will never rise up and confront it. Pride hates confrontation.

Fifth, *pride insulates you from God.*

> **The wicked, through the pride of his countenance, will not seek after God: God is not in all his thoughts.**
>
> **Psalm 10:4**

As pride insulates you from God, it brings you into self-deception (Jer. 49:16) and causes you to reject the Word of God. (Jer. 43:2.)

When the fruit of pride is fully ripened, it brings ruin.

> **Pride goeth before destruction, and an haughty spirit before a fall.**
>
> **Proverbs 16:18**

Pride is never satisfied. It always wants more, and in the end it will kill you.

Three things will help you avoid pride:

1. Remember where you were when God found you. You will stay humble when you remember where you came from and where God has brought you. You did not bring yourself there — God brought you.

2. Do not believe your own press reports. People will start "tooting your horn" when you move out in ministry, but do not believe it. Instead, believe God's report that you are a humble servant who is happy because you are obeying God. That is why everything is working right.

3. Stay close to God and make sure you give Him all the glory. That takes a conscious effort. It cannot be done subconsciously. Make the effort. It is impossible to stay close to God and stay in pride. God is too big and you cannot compete with Him. Staying close to Him will keep you humble.

Pride is not something that someone can come and lay hands on you and say, "Come out," and make you free forever. It is a daily fight. For some people, it is a moment-by-moment fight. Make the effort. Do not let pride destroy your ministry.

Killer No. 2: Money

Everybody needs money to function in the world, but it is often overrated. Money is a tool of exchange for you to use, but it is not your life. Do not confuse how much money you have with who you are.

Three problem areas can turn money into a killer, however. They are *greed, debt* and *love of money.*

Greed is the place in the soul where you have to have more, more, more, more, more — and still it is not enough. Greed will not allow you to give but causes you to want to clutch every cent and never let go. It is all right to have increase. It is all right to have money in the bank and to have a retirement account. But do not allow the spirit of greed to operate in your life. Like pride, greed can never be satisfied: it never has enough.

Concerning the second problem area, *debt,* there is a great debate about whether Christians should borrow money. This is my answer:

Yes, take out loans, but go only as far as your faith and your good conscience will allow you to go in the

Spirit of God. Do not put yourself into debt to the point where it becomes a weight or a burden on you so that what you owe monopolizes your thinking. Confusion and fear should have no place in your finances — or anywhere else, for that matter.

> **But they that will be rich fall into temptation and a snare, and into many foolish and hurtful lusts, which drown men in destruction and perdition.**
>
> **For the love of money is the root of all evil: which while some coveted after, they have erred from the faith, and pierced themselves through with many sorrows.**
>
> **1 Timothy 6:9,10**

Notice that the scripture says, **the *love* of money is the root of all evil.** It does not say that *having* money is the root of all evil. It is your attitude toward money that is important. Money does not own me; I own it. God can bless me because I give, and I like giving. God likes to prosper His people whose hearts are right.

If you find yourself lusting after money — really craving it — it is time to get your attitude adjusted before it kills you, because that is idolatry. Do not put money ahead of God.

Money often is a killer in the ministry world, because so many ministers have come out of poverty. Their families did not have much money when they were growing up. Then when their ministries grow and the money starts to come in, they do not know how to handle it. They step out of the Spirit and into the flesh, and that opens the door for the enemy to turn their blessings into cursings.

Staying close to Jesus will help you keep your heart right and your attitudes straight. Keeping Jesus first makes the other areas of your life come into the proper priority.

Killer No. 3: Sex

Financial sins are sins that come because of money. They have a short life compared to the problems that result from sexual sins. Sexual sins live. They will haunt you. The reason is because sex is the only act that can involve the creation of another soul. It is not what you might call a small, quiet sin! Sexual sin can directly affect another person's life, and indirectly, it can affect many lives. Sadly, many sexual sins involve abortion — in other words, murder.

The devil plays on a God-given physical drive and orchestrates events to put you into a position where he can push your button. If you yield when he pushes your button, he has knocked you out. If you do not know how to hold the reins on your sexual drive, it will haunt you and could eventually destroy you.

Every time you start to move forward, the enemy will say, "Remember what you did...remember?"

He wants to beat you up with the memory of what he pushed you to do in the first place.

There is only one way to avoid all of this: Get in the glory of God and stay there. Stay high in His presence. But understand this: You *can* receive forgiveness. However, if you created an "Ishmael," you will have to raise it. The consequences of the sin may not go away when forgiveness comes. Forgiveness from God wipes out the sin but does not always wipe out the consequences.

If you are not married, do not allow your emotional or physical needs to fool you into thinking you love the wrong person. Wait until you *know* from God the one you are dating is the right one. Do not go by what you think or feel. Find out from God. Participating in soulish love sets you up for hurt when the relationship breaks up — or worse, marriage to the wrong person and perhaps divorce. Stay in God's *agape* love but keep the reins on your flesh until God says, "Yes, this is the one."

If you are married, keep the lines of communication open all the time. If a problem arises, go to your spouse and both of you go to God. Work it out together. Decide together what you are going to do about the problem. Staying in agreement leaves no room for the spirit of strife and contention to enter.

Also, men, avoid the trap of taking the problem to your secretary; and women, do not take the problem to a friend of the opposite sex. That could create an emotional intimacy that might open the door to physical intimacy.

Pastors, you should not be counseling a member of the opposite sex alone. Your spouse should sit in with you. Do not create opportunites for sexual sin to enter. Build resistors inside yourself. Put chapter and verse against temptation in your heart, in order to be able to say to the devil: **It is written** (Matt. 4:7). Put the right thought patterns in there. If your mind begins to wander, wander it back where it belongs.

Say, "No, mind, you cannot think that way. I own you and I will not allow you to play with ideas like that."

Sometimes you have to speak boldly to yourself. If you do not talk to yourself, the devil will.

Otherwise, you may wake up some morning and say, "Why did I do that?" But it will be too late.

Know the devices of the devil and fight them. Particularly be aware of the three killers: pride, money and sex. Some great ministers have fallen at the height of their greatest potential for God because of these killers. It does not take twice. Once can stop your ministry for a lifetime.

Let the Devil Know Who You Are

Finally my brethren, be strong in the Lord, and in the power of his might.

Put on the whole armour of God, that ye may be able to stand against the wiles of the devil.

For we wrestle not against flesh and blood, but against principalities, against powers, against the rulers of the darkness of this world, against spiritual wickedness in high places.

Ephesians 6:10-12

Every person who obeys God is going to confront demons many times. But never forget that the Greater One lives inside you. You are a victor through Jesus Christ. You are more than a conqueror, so let the devil know it by hitting him with the power Jesus has delegated to you through His name.

Quit being nice to the devil. Get him out of your house and off your block. Do not let him give you a headache; give him one! Use the sword of the Spirit as the offensive weapon that it is. Make him worry about where you are going to hurt his kingdom next. He should be defending against your attacks instead

99

of you defending against his. Be part of God's invading force.

When you go to war, you do not go alone. God dispatches His angels to fight with you. When you step out in obedience to God, you hook up with all the other warriors of the Kingdom.

If you will walk in faith and be led by the Holy Spirit, the Lord will show you things to come. He will show you what kind of an attack the devil is going to try to mount against your home. The devil will try to tear up your marriage and destroy your children. But when you know what the plan is, you can take the battle into his territory and defeat him, before he ever gets a chance to bring the battle into your home. If the battle already is in your home, you will have to drive him out, then defend your territory to keep him from coming back.

One of the biggest secrets to having a happy home is this: Be in tune with God, and take the battle to the devil's territory in the spiritual realm.

The man of the house needs to learn that being on his knees before the Lord is a position of manhood. The whole family needs to band together in spiritual warfare, but the man should take the most responsibility.

The Reality of Warfare

The Lord burned a picture of the reality of warfare into my mind when He sent me to Africa. We were not playing "cowboys and Indians." It was real. The Lord sent us to a little Assemblies of God church in Zobo, a city in the communist nation of Mozambique. He sent me to teach them how to fight demons.

Mozambique was in a state of civil war, with rebels fighting against the nation's communist troops. We traveled as part of a Zimbabwe army convoy that had to cross Mozambique to carry supplies between Zimbabwe and Malawi. We headed for Zobo right through some of the areas where the heaviest fighting had been taking place.

I thought, "If anything is going to happen, it will happen on the way over."

So I sat in the front of the truck to watch and pray. Praise God, nothing happened. I preached that night, and early the next morning we caught the convoy back. I got in the back of the truck this time, so I could lie down and sleep. About 6:35 a.m., gunfire started. I was an American teenager at the time who knew nothing about guns or gunfire. I just turned over and went back to sleep.

When the gunfire got closer, someone hit the back of the truck and said, "Get up! Get out!"

So I got up and sat on the back of the truck and looked around. I turned to my associate, Scott, and said, "This is just like television. Look at this!"

That was not one of the most intelligent things I have ever done. I thought the battle was down the road, when in fact we were right in the middle of the crossfire! And our white skin made us stand out like neon signs in the morning light. One of the Zimbabwe soldiers was hit and killed. Finally I realized that we were not in a game, and that we could no longer stay there in the middle of the road and be amused by machine gun bullets clipping the bushes.

I got a revelation of the reality of the situation, but we had not been trained in physical warfare. So we just walked over and sat down in the ditch, when we should have *run* and jumped in the ditch as soon as we left the truck. The Mozambique rebels shooting at the convoy were trying to capture supplies because they were starving.

One of them came up on top of us, and I thought, "Lord, are You there?"

Fear tried to grip my heart. If you allow fear to grip you, you are in big trouble. *Never react in the natural; respond in the spirit.* That is an important key in spiritual warfare. Do not touch it in the natural or with your mind. Let your spirit respond.

I did not have time to pull out a faith tape or remember a formula. If I had tried to remember every faith outline I had heard or preached, I would have died.

What my spirit responded with was Psalm 62:8.

Trust in him at all times; ye people, pour out your heart before him: God is a refuge for us. Selah.

I had to trust God and allow Him to be my refuge. I could not pick up a gun and fight, because I did not know how.

Eventually the fighting ceased, and it was only a miracle of God that we were still alive. The rebel had disappeared as suddenly as he had appeared. Our ignorance easily could have cost us our lives, and that is the point of my story: *Many people approach spiritual warfare the way I approached the battle in the natural.*

At first it seems like fun, like a game. It seems unreal until the first time you really take a blow. Do not go into spiritual warfare with an attitude of playing games. Realize that the fight is real, so that you will attack and not suffer when you get in a battle. You will know what is going on and respond, instead of wandering around in a daze of unreality.

On the way out of that incident, God said, "I wanted you to see where my Church stands today. I wanted you to experience how my believers stand today. I wanted you to sense the fear, to see the torture, to see the death that happens in the world of the spirit for those who do not know how to fight the devil.

"So what you saw in the natural is what happens in the spiritual realm every single day on earth. I see them die. I see them shot. I see them out there playing games, not taking it as real. My Kingdom suffers. My people are lost because they are not seeing reality. They think it is a game. It *is* imaginary to some.

"But I want you to know that the battle we are in is real. People suffer. People die spiritually because you do not pray, because you do not fight. It is real out here in the spiritual realm. The talk of being in a war is true. It is not a figure of speech."

Obedience Threatens the Enemy

The closer you walk to God, the more understanding of spiritual battles you will have. When you obey God in the world of the spirit, you threaten and harm the powers of the devil. A Christian in the natural does not threaten the devil like an obedient believer does in the spirit world.

When you really step out into that realm, you become a big target for the devil, because you can hurt him. Nearly everywhere you go you will be in a battle. I travel at least twenty days out of the month and go from one battle to another.

Far too many churches have no awareness of the battle in the spiritual realm, so demons have a free rein over them. I have to fight a battle just to get into the pulpit and preach in some places. The glory is a weapon, too. You can pray until the glory falls, and it will scare the devil out of the place.

We have to fight the good fight of faith, and that fight is not in the natural. We do not fight against other people. We battle principalities and powers and wicked spirits in heavenly places.

Pick Up the Weapons

Be strong in the power of His might, and pick up the weapons God has given you. Make Him glad that you are a part of His army. When you accept Christ as your personal Savior, you go into boot camp. When you learn the lessons of boot camp, you go to war. Then there are those who go into special training. They have the goal of becoming the Green Berets of the Spirit.

Instead of walking around and sowing strife, the Green Berets of the Spirit sow truth. They encourage people in the faith. Soon there is no discord when people get together. They start shouting and praying, the glory falls, and the devil has lost again.

The prophets of God are coming, and they are like spies. They go in behind the battle lines and sneak into the enemy's headquarters. They steal the code books and the strategy books.

They come back to the Church with those plans and say, "This is what the enemy plans to do, and this is how God says we should stop it."

The Lord recently told me, "I've given the Church many weapons. But they never read the manual on how to use them. That's why they are being shot to death while they are holding the most powerful weapon in the universe in their hands. They don't know how to shoot, because they don't read the manual."

It is time that we learn how to shoot our spiritual guns. It is time that we launch the demon-seeking missiles in the spirit. It is time to go out to battle.

Too many Christians today think they are on vacation, while the world is crumbling all around them. There are no furloughs in God's army. Get into the battle and win. Drive the enemy out of your territory, then go looking for new territory to conquer.

Paul's Example

The Apostle Paul fought many spiritual battles. Look at this one in chapter 16 of Acts.

> And it came to pass, as we went to prayer, a certain damsel possessed with a spirit of divination met us, which brought her masters much gain by soothsaying:
>
> The same followed Paul and us, and cried, saying, These men are the servants of the most high God, which shew unto us the way of salvation.

> And this did she many days. But Paul, being grieved, turned and said to the spirit, I command thee in the name of Jesus Christ to come out of her. And he came out the same hour.
>
> Acts 16:16-18

Notice that Paul did not react; he responded in the Spirit. He did not come against the woman herself. He launched his attack against the demon in her and drove it out of her. But when you cast out an evil spirit, all the other demons in the vicinity know about it. Sometimes they get together and counterattack.

> And when her masters saw that the hope of their gains was gone, they caught Paul and Silas, and drew them into the marketplace unto the rulers,
>
> And brought them to the magistrates, saying, These men, being Jews, do exceedingly trouble our city,
>
> And teach customs, which are not lawful for us to receive, neither to observe, being Romans.
>
> And the multitude rose up together against them: and the magistrates rent off their clothes, and commanded to beat them.
>
> And when they had laid many stripes upon them, they cast them into prison, charging the jailor to keep them safely:
>
> Who, having received such a charge, thrust them into the inner prison, and made their feet fast in the stocks.
>
> And at midnight Paul and Silas prayed, and sang praises unto God: and the prisoners heard them.
>
> And suddenly there was a great earthquake, so that the foundations of the prison were shaken: and immediately all the doors were opened, and every one's bands were loosed.
>
> Acts 16:19-26

The demons counterattacked by having the girl's masters stir up the crowds and the local magistrates. Paul and Silas were severely beaten and thrown into prison, but they did not despair. They were prisoners of war, but they did not stay that way long. They sang and praised God, joyfully continuing the battle. And God supernaturally delivered them.

If you get captured when you obediently go into spiritual warfare, God will not leave you as a prisoner of war for long. Keep your attitude right. Stay in the joy and the peace of the Lord, and He will deliver you and take you into victory.

Believe God. Fight the devils. Praise God and enjoy the victory.

8

The Power of Godly Confrontation

The word *confrontation* makes a lot of Christians nervous. When the word is used in the context of fighting devils, it does not bother them. But when *confrontation* is used in connection with training and personal growth, they do not like it. People tend to resist change, *but God expects us to change.*

But we all, with open face beholding as in a glass the glory of the Lord, are *changed* into the same image from glory to glory, even as by the Spirit of the Lord.
2 Corinthians 3:18

God's plan is for us to be *changed* into the image of Christ. We are to be like Him in spirit, soul and body. However, our souls and bodies will not change unless they are confronted with the difference between God's ideal and our current reality. The same thing applies to churches. Change will not come without confrontation.

Confrontation can come in a variety of ways, ranging from a gentle hint to a bold word that hits hard. How it comes, when it comes, and through whom it comes should all be directed by the Holy Spirit.

In recent decades, the Body of Christ has replaced godly confrontation with gushy, sloppy, soulish love — a perverted love. If we keep walking in this gushy stuff, we will not prevail, and we will not avail much for the Kingdom of God.

There is a powerful sweet anointing and a powerful bold anointing. Both are from God, but if you only accept one of them, you will have a problem. If you stay stuck in the sweet, you will never know the bold. If you stay stuck in the bold, you will never know the sweet. You need to know how to flow back and forth between the two as the Spirit leads.

If you are already uncomfortable with this chapter, please do not quit reading now. I have found that the sermons I least like are the ones I need the most. Your mind and emotions fight change. They feel anything that brings change is an attack and a threat.

> **For the word of God is quick, and powerful, and sharper than any twoedged sword, piercing even to the dividing asunder of soul and spirit, and of the joints and marrow, and is a discerner of the thoughts and intents of the heart.**
>
> **Hebrews 4:12**

The Word of God is sharp and powerful. Properly applied, it can set people free. On the other hand, if it is not used properly, it can wound and kill. The person applying the Word *must* be led by the Spirit. I cannot emphasize that enough.

Many people have been wounded or worse by soulish Christians wielding the sword of the Word like an ax, who have hacked people to death. That sword needs to be handled as a skillful surgeon uses a scalpel to cut out a cancerous growth and still leave everything around it untouched.

Sometimes, ministers see a problem and just go after it. While we are killing it, we are mutilating everything else, so there is nothing left when we get through. Some preachers have lost their ministries because they were undisciplined surgeons. They operated without the discipline and training of the Spirit, leaving a trail of mutilated people. Eventually they got called on God's carpet for malpractice, for abusing the sheep.

The Bible gives many examples of Spirit-led confrontation.

John the Baptist

> In those days came John the Baptist, preaching in the wilderness of Judaea,
>
> And saying, Repent ye: for the kingdom of heaven is as hand.
>
> For this is he that was spoken of by the prophet Esaias, saying, The voice of one crying in the wilderness, Prepare ye the way of the Lord, make his paths straight.
>
> John 3:1-3

How do you prepare the way of Lord? How do you make crooked paths straight? You cannot just look at them; you have to confront them. Crooked paths are those we make to keep our flesh comfortable, so we will not have to give up anything as we travel down the spiritual path.

> And the same John had his raiment of camel's hair, and a leathern girdle about his loins; and his meat was locusts and wild honey.
>
> Then went out to him Jerusalem, and all Judaea, and all the region round about Jordan,
>
> And were baptized of him in Jordan, confessing their sins.

> **But when he saw many of the Pharisees and Sadducees** (in other words, religious devils) **come to his baptism, he said unto them, O generation of vipers, who hath warned you to flee from the wrath to come?**
>
> **Bring forth therefore fruits meet for repentance:**
>
> **And think not to say within yourselves, We have Abraham for our father: for I say unto you, that God is able of these stones to raise up children unto Abraham.**
>
> **And now also the ax is laid unto the root of the trees: therefore every tree which bringeth not forth good fruit is hewn down, and cast into the fire.**
>
> John 3:4-10

John the Baptist was called to confrontation: "Repent and be baptized." His call was not one that would be soulishly acceptable to a lot of people today. But it is spiritually acceptable to all those who are hungering and thirsting after righteousness, to those who want to be changed into the image of Christ.

Every sermon should be confrontive. Every sermon should challenge you.

If you are confronted and hungry to have the Word working in your life, you will be happy. If the sermon confronts a sin, you will grow sad until you repent and feel the cleansing power of God flow through you. But if you do not want correction, you will get mad.

When I go into a church for the first time, I do not know anything about the congregation. As I start preaching the Gospel by the leading of the Holy Spirit, I can see how the Word is hitting them by the way they react. I hope for happy faces, but in a lot of churches, I see straight faces, sad faces, or angry eyebrows. I keep trying to tell them I am a nice guy, but they do not like me when I hit a "pet" flesh area they are in agreement with.

If ministers will not keep putting the Word out to confront sin, weakness, and wrong, the people will never grow up and be changed into His image. We have too many congregations today who cannot weather even the smallest storms. When they get into the slightest battle, they collapse into a wimpering mass of jelly. How can they stand against the enemy like that? They cannot. So the enemy spreads them on toast and eats them for breakfast. We *must* be willing to change and grow!

Love Confronts

Some people have the idea that the love of God never deals with things. But the love of God is not a nonchalant force. It is a direct, confrontive force that reveals right and wrong, because no evil shall be found in the presence of God.

The first thing God did in creation was separate *light* from *darkness*. God's love confronts wrong things in our lives, so we can recognize them and choose to change. We have to *choose* to change, because God will not come against our wills.

Look at an example from Jesus' life.

And they (Jesus and the disciples) **come to Jerusalem: and Jesus went into the temple, and began to cast out them that sold and bought in the temple, and overthrew the tables of the moneychangers, and the seats of them that sold doves;**

> And would not suffer that any man should carry any vessel through the temple.
>
> And he taught, saying unto them, Is it not written, My house shall be called of all nations the house of prayer? but ye have made it a den of thieves.
>
> And the scribes and chief priests heard it, and sought how they might destroy him: for they feared him, because all the people was astonished at his doctrine.
>
> And when even was come, he went out of the city.
>
> Mark 11:15-19

When Jesus walked into the Temple, His spirit rose up strong and went after those who had begun to make a mockery of the Temple. He physically threw them out. No wimp would have been able to do that! Was He walking in love when He did it? Absolutely. The love in Him confronted the wrong in the Temple, then He taught them what was right.

The same thing applies to us as individuals and as the Church. We are the temple of the Holy Spirit, and the love of God will confront the wrong things in us and teach us the right things.

Now you might say, "Those people's hearts were right. It was not nice for Jesus to toss them out on their ears."

However, your heart can be right and your actions totally wrong. God deals with both. The fact that you have a nice heart does not mean God will let your actions continue to be wrong. He wants both of them to conform to His image.

Confrontation can be taken three ways:

Some people will completely reject the truth of the confrontation and be like the scribes and chief priests who wanted to kill Jesus for cleaning the Temple.

Others will accept the truth of the confrontation but try to avoid any real changes by making excuses.

"You don't know what I've been through in my life."

Quit finding excuses for your flesh! Also, learn to know the difference between what is your own soul and what is demonic influence. If you can choose to do or not do whatever the problem is, more than likely, it is coming from flesh. However, if the problem or the attitude is hardened and even verges on dogmatism, obsession, or compulsion — then you more than likely are being influenced by a demon.

The right way to deal with confrontation is to accept truth and change. There may not be an immediate change, but at least there should be a strong commitment to change. That will get you on the right track. Some things can be changed instantly, some take time.

I know the world needs love, but I believe it needs "godly tough love." That is the love that will go out in the ditch and pull you out. It is not the "nice love" that says, "I don't want to get dirty. You send someone else." Tough love will lift you up out of a ditch, and it will sit you down and show you where you need to change. Then it will help you change.

The Holy Spirit's perfect way of confronting problems in us is by the inward witness. He will continue trying to reach us through the inward witness until we change or become dull of hearing in our hearts. Then, I believe, He will bring someone to us — an outside voice — to make a very strong impression on our spirits or our souls.

When you are dull of hearing or dull of seeing and the Holy Spirit must bring an outside pressure, the obedient person who talks to you may not know what he is doing. I have had that happen to me several times. Someone would say something to me, and it would prick my heart. They would not know it, but I would think, "Hey, God is trying to get to me. I'd better listen here."

Truth Offends Soulish People

Walking in the Spirit keeps you from being offended by the truth of God's Word. If you are walking in the soul, you probably will be offended many times when the truth comes.

The religious leaders of Jesus' time had a difficult time accepting the truth from Him. Chapter 8 of John records a lengthy confrontation between them.

> **Then spake Jesus again unto them, saying, I am the light of the world: he that followeth me shall not walk in darkness, but shall have the light of life.**
>
> **The Pharisees therefore said unto him, Thou bearest record of thyself; thy record is not true.**
> **John 8:12,13**

The Pharisees said Jesus was lying. He continued to speak the truth to them, and they continued to challenge it. They could not understand it.

Then said Jesus again unto them, I go my way, and ye shall seek me, and shall die in your sins: whither I go, ye cannot come.

Then said the Jews, Will he kill himself? because he saith, Whither I go, ye cannot come.

And he said unto them, Ye are from beneath; I am from above: ye are of this world; I am not of this world.

I said therefore unto you, that ye shall die in your sins: for if ye believe not that I am he, ye shall die in your sins.

Then said they unto him, Who art thou? And Jesus saith unto them, Even the same that I said unto you from the beginning.

I have many things to say and to judge of you: but he that sent me is true; and I speak to the world those things which I have heard of him.

They understood not that he spake to them of the Father.

John 8:21-27

When the truth comes, the soulish person throws up strong defenses to deflect it or misunderstand it, because the soul hates to change. The soul will deny the truth and challenge the one who delivers it by saying, "Who do you think you are to be correcting me? What right do you have to say that? Who made you judge over me?"

The soulish walls of the religious leaders were high and thick, but Jesus kept hitting them with the truth in the hopes that something would finally get through their defenses and prick their hearts, so they could repent.

> But now ye seek to kill me, a man that hath told you the truth, which I have heard of God: this did not Abraham.
>
> Ye do the deeds of your father. Then said they to him, We be not born of fornication; we have one Father, even God.
>
> Jesus said unto them, If God were your Father, ye would love me: for I proceeded forth and came from God; neither came I of myself, but he sent me.
>
> Why do you not understand my speech? even because ye cannot hear my word.
>
> Ye are of your father the devil, and the lusts of your father ye will do. He was a murderer from the beginning, and abode not in the truth, because there is no truth in him. When he speaketh a lie, he speaketh of his own: for he is a liar, and the father of it.
>
> And because I tell you the truth, ye believe me not.
>
> John 8:40-45

Jesus confronted them with bold words, direct words, hard-hitting words. There were no political (diplomatic) words spoken.

He did not say, "What you're doing reminds me of a little story...."

When the soulish walls are firmly in place, a hint will not do. Only a bold, frontal attack can break through the hardness of the heart and the deafness of the ears.

A friend once told me, "There are so many roots in people's lives that are not of God. It takes bold words and confrontive people to knock those roots out of people, so they can get re-rooted in the Word and produce good fruit."

Roots of pride, roots of rejection, roots of fear, roots of rebellion, roots of self-will, roots of bitterness, roots of offendedness — the list can go on and on. It often takes a bold, anointed word coming from the heart of God to go, "BAM," and pull those roots out.

Jeremiah — the Confrontive Prophet

The prophet Jeremiah was anointed to confront problems and root them out.

> But the Lord said unto me, Say not, I am a child: for thou shalt go to all that I shall send thee, and whatsoever I command thee thou shalt speak.
>
> Be not afraid of their faces: for I am with thee to deliver thee, saith the Lord.
>
> Then the Lord put forth his hand, and touched my mouth. And the Lord said unto me, Behold, I have put my words in thy mouth.
>
> See, I have this day set thee over the nations and over the kingdoms, to root out, and to pull down, and to destroy, and to throw down, to build, and to plant.
>
> Jeremiah 1:7-10

Everything in that last verse is a forward push. It takes confrontiveness to root out, pull down, and destroy. It also takes confrontiveness to build and plant. Verse 9 holds the key to the strength of Jeremiah's ministry: The words of the Lord were in his mouth. God's confrontiveness roots *out* and plants. It pulls out the wrong and plants the right. Confrontiveness without the word of the Lord, without His prompting and direction, destroys without building up. *We must be led by the Spirit.*

In chapter 23, Jeremiah confronted problems in Israel that were like the problems in the Church today.

> Woe be unto the pastors that destroy and scatter the sheep of my pasture! saith the Lord.
>
> Therefore thus saith the Lord God of Israel against the pastors that feed my people; Ye have scattered my flock, and driven them away, and have not visited them: behold, I will visit upon you the evil of your doings, saith the Lord.
>
> And I will gather the remnant of my flock out of all countries whither I have driven them, and will bring them again to their folds; and they shall be fruitful and increase.
>
> And I will set up shepherds over them which shall feed them: and they shall fear no more, nor be dismayed, neither shall they be lacking, saith the Lord.
>
> **Jeremiah 23:1-4**

Here God was using Jeremiah to confront the pastors who were hirelings instead of shepherds. Pastors who fail to feed and protect the flocks entrusted to them by God will be removed and replaced by those who will be obedient. We are seeing it today. God will not allow the sheep to be fleeced and scattered anymore.

Spiritual leaders must be led by the Spirit. A pastor who confronts his flock out of his soul instead of the Spirit will scatter them. A pastor who walks in love and confronts when and how God says to confront will root out and plant. God will bless that pastor. Failing to confront when God says to will hurt the flock as well.

If God is trying to clean up problems in a church and the leaders are going around saying, "Everything is fine...there are no problems here...peace and blessings on everyone," those leaders are creating a false sense of security in the flock.

A flock will not change and grow under those circumstances. Those leaders are standing in the way of God's move instead of flowing with it in obedience.

A few verses later, we see Jeremiah confronting the disobedient prophets and priests. God wanted holiness and obedience in Jeremiah's day, and He wants it now!

> My heart within me is broken because of the prophets; all my bones shake; I am like a drunken man, and like a man whom wine hath overcome, because of the Lord, and because of the words of his holiness.
>
> For the land is full of adulterers; for because of swearing the land mourneth; the pleasant places of the wilderness are dried up, and their course is evil, and their force is not right.
>
> For both prophet and priest are profane; yea, in my house have I found their wickedness, saith the Lord.
>
> Wherefore their way shall be unto them as slippery ways in the darkness: they shall be driven on, and fall therein: for I will bring evil upon them, even the year of their visitation, saith the Lord.
>
> And I have seen folly in the prophets of Samaria; they prophesied in Baal, and caused my people Israel to err.
>
> I have seen also in the prophets of Jerusalem an horrible thing: they commit adultery, and walk in lies: they strengthen also the hands of evildoers, that none

doth return from his wickedness: they are all of them unto me as Sodom, and the inhabitants thereof as Gomorrah.

Therefore thus saith the Lord of hosts concerning the prophets; Behold I will feed them with wormwood, and make them drink the water of gall: for from the prophets of Jerusalem is profaneness gone forth into all the land.

Thus saith the Lord of hosts, Hearken not unto the words of the prophets that prophesy unto you: they make you vain: they speak a vision of their own heart, and not out of the mouth of the Lord.

They say still unto them that despise me, The Lord hath said, Ye shall have peace; and they say unto every one that walketh after the imagination of his own heart, No evil shall come upon you.

For who hath stood in the counsel of the Lord, and hath perceived and heard his word? who hath marked his word, and heard it?

Behold, a whirlwind of the Lord is gone forth in fury, even a grievous whirlwind: it shall fall grievously upon the head of the wicked.

The anger of the Lord shall not return, until he have executed, and till he have performed the thoughts of his heart: in the latter days ye shall consider it perfectly.

I have not sent these prophets, yet they ran: I have not spoken to them, yet they prophesied.

But if they had stood in my counsel, and had caused my people to hear my words, then they should have turned them from their evil way, and from the evil of their doings.

Jeremiah 23:9-22

The people will turn from their evil ways if the spiritual leaders will listen to the word of the Lord and then speak it.

Paul's Example

The Apostle Paul regularly confronted the wrong in the churches through his epistles and in person. He also confronted the other leaders when it was necessary.

> But when Peter was come to Antioch, I withstood him to his face, because he was to be blamed.
>
> For before that certain came from James, he did eat with the Gentiles: but when they were come, he withdrew and separated himself, fearing them which were of the circumcision.
>
> And the other Jews dissembled likewise with him; insomuch that Barnabas also was carried away with their dissimulation.
>
> But when I saw that they walked not uprightly according to the truth of the gospel, I said unto Peter before them all, If thou, being a Jew, livest after the manner of Gentiles, and not as do the Jews, why compellest thou the Gentiles to live as do the Jews?
>
> We who are Jews by nature, and not sinners of the Gentiles,
>
> Knowing that a man is not justified by the works of the law, but by the faith of Jesus Christ, even we have believed in Jesus Christ, that we might be justified by the faith of Christ, and not by the works of the law: for by the works of the law shall no flesh be justified.
>
> **Galatians 2:11-16**

Paul confronted Peter face to face. He did not backbite and grumble about him behind his back. He boldly confronted the wrong so Peter and the others could grow and change.

Confrontation is a major part of the new move of God, because holiness will not come without it. We have been able to get away with some things in the past but not in this new move. Jesus is looking for a Bride without spot or wrinkle, and we will never get into that place unless we confront the unholiness in our lives and get it out. We must bring every area of life into absolute obedience to God and His Word.

9

The Church Must Walk in Authority

Authority must come back into the pulpits of North America, not soulish strength, but spiritual authority. We have begun to see the strength of God come forth. It is in those who are walking by the Spirit and living in the authority and the command of God. Those who are concerned about everyone else's opinions will not walk in spiritual authority.

Devils hate authority. They love soulish talk and religious talk, because there is no real authority being exercised over them. You can see that happening in the ministry of Jesus: He went to a synagogue in Capernaum one Saturday during the Sabbath service, and His authority caused a demon to get stirred up.

> **And they were astonished at his doctrine: for he taught them as one that had authority, and not as the scribes.**
>
> **And there was in their synagogue a man who had an unclean spirit; and he cried out,**
>
> **Saying, Let us alone; what have we to do with thee, thou Jesus of Nazareth? art come to destroy us? I know thee who thou art, the Holy One of God.**
>
> **And Jesus rebuked him, saying, Hold thy peace, and come out of him.**
>
> **Mark 1:22-25**

The point I want to make is that healing and deliverance flow together. They go together. Look at Acts 10:38:

> **How God anointed Jesus of Nazareth with the Holy Ghost and with power: who went about doing good, and *healing all that were oppressed of the devil; for God was with him.***

There is coming a great surge of deliverance. Before we hit the revival, there will be a clean-up time in order for the glorious Church to get glorious. One way to get cleaned up is through deliverance. The revival is not a deliverance revival, but it has deliverance as part of it. I also feel there will come a time, as we move into the greater glory of God, when there will be reactions to that glory. Demons on people in the services will manifest. So what do you do? You take care of them, and go on. You do not exalt deliverance; you exalt the Deliverer.

Many Things Will Be Revealed

The Spirit is being poured out on all flesh in a greater dimension. And when the Holy Spirit hits flesh, what happens? Whatever is in that person will react to the Spirit. If God is strong in him, he will react positively to the presence of God. If a demon is on or in him, it will react in resistance.

Every church in North America needs to allow the voice of God to come to them again in deliverance. People called into healing ministries who do not want to cast out devils will not see the magnitude of what their ministries could be. Strong healing and strong deliverance should be a way of life to any minister who wants to be part of what God is doing.

You do not *wash* devils by the Word. You wash the individual. Devils are not going to be cleansed. You *cast out* devils. Some of them will leave through the *preaching* of the Word, but what we are facing in the harvest coming into the Church is a great need for deliverance.

We are dealing with a class of devils who plan their strategy and wait for the ideal time to cause a fall. Then the demon will hinder through the memory of that fall. (Ephesians 6:12 tells us that there are different types and levels of devils: principalities, powers, rulers of the darkness of this world, spiritual wickedness in high places.)

Believers are being raised up with anointings to take cities and nations, not just one block. However, if some are not taken through deliverance, they will rise *and* fall, because they will not be able to live on track with God. The devil is trying to put them in bondage and break them, but Jesus wants them free.

Home Life Is of Great Importance

From my study of great men and women of God in the past, I have learned their home lives were of major importance. Devils go after children because they are vulnerable. If parents do not provide spiritual protection and covering, children are more vulnerable.

I was raised in a very godly and powerful home. There were many things common to my home that I found later were not normal in other people's homes. One was fighting the devil. I could walk home from school, come in the front door, and if something was not right, guess what? My parents or my grandparents would grab me and cast that spirit off. After that I was fine.

Pentecostal-Charismatic Witchcraft

Another problem today is what I call "Pentecostal-Charismatic witchcraft." That is people who love the Lord in Full Gospel churches, but who are not in the realm of the Holy Spirit. They get out there in the soul and end up running around with familiar spirits and having visions that do not come from heaven. The Church must learn to deal with this in bold and plain ways.

In these cases, a pastor should not say, "Let's pray for them."

He should get that spirit off them so they can be free from bondage.

Also, I want you to be aware that people in the fivefold offices are not immune to soulish operations or demonic influence:

- A pastor who gets in the flesh becomes someone who controls.

- An evangelist who gets in the flesh goes "Hollywood."

- A teacher who gets in the flesh simply gives out information with no anointing and can get critical of other people who do not say things exactly the same way.

- A prophet who gets into the flesh gets "spacey" or judgmental.

- An apostle who gets into the flesh gets legalistic and prideful.

Maria Woodworth-Etter, the well-known evangelist from the turn of the century, said, "At the same time God gives me a gift of the Holy Spirit, the devil tries to give me a false one."

The Devil Offers False "Gifts"

The operations of the prophet and apostle are going to be revealed in greater authority than we have ever seen before. After the Spirit begins to move, we will see things pulled down, destroyed, and thrown away. The proper building and planting will be done. Ideas of devils and men will be blasted.

Musicians and singers will operate in a deeper dimension of the Spirit as well as the fivefold offices. God is invading every part of our lives and ministries, and He wants to rearrange the music departments of our churches. We have lost great musicians and singers to the secular music industry because we would not allow the Spirit of God to move, because we would not instruct them, or because they would not receive instruction.

Even musicians and singers will need to learn discernment, because *with a special anointing comes responsibility.* Many people want the action, but they do not want the responsibility. The responsibility of the power and the glory is great. It is not a game! If you do not take the responsibility, you will lose the anointing.

One of the greatest reasons people get into error is that if they lose the real anointing, they reach out and get a false one. Because someone produces a sign and wonder does not always mean it is from God. If my spirit witnesses something wrong with a minister, yet there are still miracles going on — I will not go near that man. I have sense enough to go by my spirit and not my head.

The Church must wake up to the presence of the demonic because, in days to come, there will be the false as well as the real anointed performing signs and wonders. You cannot go by what you see.

Christians need to learn to be careful. There are false ministries coming.

Stay Where God Puts You

One reason why so many people have not been able to grow spiritually is because they do not stay in one church long enough to get what God wants them to get. They run to this seminar or to that special speaker, or they run to hear someone else prophesy. And they keep running. God will follow for a while, very patiently. Then those who run will lose their joy. The cloud of the Spirit is on the place where God wanted them to stay — and they are not in it.

When God causes someone to prophesy, the word is for those who stay in that place, not for those who run from place to place. Quit being a "church hopper," if that is what you have been doing. Find out where God wants you to stay, and stay there regardless of circumstances. You can get deceived by running to and fro.

Holiness Required Today

Another thing is that you cannot keep sinning on Saturday nights and expect to be blessed on Sunday mornings. The devil is going to throw sinful thoughts at you, but learn to cast them down. In this next move, you will need to live in holiness to get blessed.

If God required holiness in the days written of in the book of Acts, if He required holiness in the early days of the creation of the world, He requires it today. No matter what generation you are of or how you were raised, when God says something, it is so. When He says we must live holy, then we had better begin living holy!

Holiness is important. If you do not live holy, you will not live long in the glory. What we need today is the Word of God coming from the mouths of His ministers in such holiness that it will cause action in the pews.

You are going to see a great coming together in the Body of Christ.

The atmosphere is so important, no matter where you go. It must complement the Holy Spirit. You must build an environment where He likes to dwell. You must keep it clean from devils and clean from flesh. Get in the world of the Holy Spirit, and learn to operate.

A good environment now will save you much trouble and pain later. It can keep you from falling. This new move of God is a move of action, not discussion.

A good environment is one that is cleansed of the world, the flesh, and the devil. Many ministers who do believe in deliverance today have the idea that a "good environment" is one where demons come out nice and quietly. That is not the case. A good environment is one where demons come out and leave. Period.

Most people do not want demons to holler when they come out. Somehow the Church has gotten the idea that if demons holler, then the one doing the deliverance is not spiritually strong. If you read the New Testament, you will see that demons cast out by Jesus yelled on their way out. If He had it in His ministry, we certainly are going to have it in ours at times.

In the Garden of Eden, Adam and Eve realized they were naked and hid when God came asking, "Where are you?"

Today, God is still coming and asking ministers, "Where are you?"

And many of them are not where they are supposed to be! Many are not wearing their spiritual clothing. They do not have the right anointing. If you do not have the fresh anointing, you do not have on spiritual clothing.

It is time to get your environment straightened out so that you can walk in boldness.

Exercise Authority in Boldness

It is time to invade the devil's territory. Do not be ashamed of the Gospel. Do not be ashamed of the revelations that God gives you. If you make a mistake, admit it, ask everyone to forgive you, and go on. Take your God-given authority and use it.

In a church service, if the pastor turns it over to me, it is my responsibility to keep things in order. If people begin to do things that are not right, it is up to me to exercise authority and do what I am supposed to do with it.

If demons begin to act up in a service, take your God-given, Jesus-delegated authority and cast them out. You must learn to walk in authority and not feel guilty. I had to learn how to look at people and tell them to stop, for what they were doing was not right. I had to learn to tell them to sit down, and I had to learn not to feel guilty. Exercising spiritual authority is not domination.

You need to become ruthless in faith to become an invading force. You need to cause the world of the spirit to know who you are in Christ. Be brave in faith. Stir up the gift of God that is within you and walk in holy boldness.

If the world ever needed healing and deliverance ministries, it needs them now. The Church needs them.

Conclusion

God is cleansing His Church. He is going to have a spotless and clean Church, one without sin and without demons.

God's plan is that nations will be changed, and cities will become places of spiritual greatness, not of perversion. He has places in the country that are no longer "nice teaching centers," but are becoming militant schools to train soldiers of the cross. Soldiers are being sent out to blast the devil, to establish truth, and to make the name of the Lord be the salvation of the cities and towns where they are.

It is exciting to be a part of that. This is the day when all things shall come to pass. Another word of the Lord came for the Body not long ago that pertains to this time:

> Rearrangments are coming to the righteous people of the earth — rearrangements of lifestyles and goals. Plans that have been made shall be altered, saith the Spirit of the Lord.

> They have planned to move this way and to function that way, but *My* plan shall interrupt their plans and rearrangements shall come even of the anointings that they carry at this hour — the anointings in which many have grown comfortable shall no longer produce for them as they have in the past. I have

a fresh plan and a fresh power and a fresh anointing for all who are of My name. But they must realize it and accept it and begin to flow in it in a very zealous way.

This is the day when the way in which the youth flow also shall be arranged. Many of them have planned for this and for that, but their learning shall speed up and the growth of their inner men also shall speed up. They shall be young, yet old, and they will stand in positions of authority and lead masses while the age of the bodies in which they live are yet young.

Marriages shall take on a new look and a new flow. The way children are trained in the home also will be different. No longer will children be just nice little boys or girls who play with toys that you buy, but they shall be children who pray and sing and do the work of the Lord while they are yet young.

Many say, "I want to run this way" (be a part of this that God is doing), but there are things that hold them bound, weighed down. But there has come a time when such things will be broken. Weights and anchors will fall. Men's minds will become pure again. Men's hearts will become strong, beating with the Gospel way.

The young and the old shall flow together as one. There will not be two individual camps, but there shall be one.

And there shall be rearrangements of desires inside of many. This is the day when I will make even those crooked places straight, says the Lord. I will cause the desires of the hearts and of the flesh to come out in the right (alignment). Things you know are wrong, yet cannot seem to do anything about, the Spirit of the Lord will come upon and correct and rearrange and readjust and heal those things that need to be taken care of.

Do you want to be part of God's revival? Or do you want to just stay in the old? Now is the time to make your choice.

The hour of God has dawned. Be a part — do your part, and God will do His part.

Roberts Liardon Ministries International Sales Contacts:

In England, Europe, Eastern Europe, and Scandanavia
P.O. Box 103
Knutsford
Cheshire WA169EL
England

In Asia:
Roberts Liardon Productions
Ruffles City
P.O. Box 1365
Singapore 9117

In New Zealand and Australia:
Lifeway Ministries
P.O. Box 303
Warkworth, New Zealand

Additional copies of this book and other books and videos,
are available from your local bookstore or by contacting:

Embassy Publishing
P.O. Box 3500
Laguna Hills, CA 92654

Other Books by Roberts Liardon

Kathryn Kuhlman
A Spiritual Biography of God's Miracle Working Power
Learning To Say No Without Feeling Guilty
I Saw Heaven
A Call To Action
The Invading Force
The Quest for Spiritual Hunger
The Price of Spiritual Power
Breaking Controlling Powers
Religious Politics
Cry of the Spirit
Spiritual Timing

Videos by Roberts Liardon

I Saw Heaven
God's Explosive Weapons
The Roar of the '90s
The Sword of Gideon
Developing an Excellent Spirit
No More Walls
Confronting the Brazen Heavens
Invasion '91 (10-tape series)
Reformers and Revivalists (5-volume series)
God's Generals
(8-volume set of tapes, 60 minutes each)

To contact Roberts Liardon
write:

Roberts Liardon Ministries
P.O. Box 30710
Laguna Hills, CA 92654

Please include your prayer requests and comments when you write.

Spirit Life Journal is Roberts Liardon's "pulpit to the world." Each colorful, bi-monthly issue will challenge, encourage and enlighten you with faith-building articles on God's past "Generals," Guest Pulpit articles from ministers around the world; plus special messages and features from Roberts.

For your free subscription, write:

ROBERTS LIARDON MINISTRIES
P.O. Box 30710
Laguna Hills, CA 92654-0710

(Be sure to print your complete address, zip code or country code).

REVIVAL TO THE NATIONS

A New Generation Bringing Revival To The Nations

Spirit Life Bible College
Laguna Hills, California

It is the heart of Life Bible Scool to raise and train a generation of people to go out and subdue the hardened spiritual climate of a nation, and win it for the Kingdom of God. We will train our students how to live victoriously in any environment, emerging with the message, the joy and the life of God.

Roberts Liardon
Founder & President

Some of the courses include:

Spiritual Leadership	God's Generals
Gifts of the Spirit	Human Illness & Healing
Soul Development/The Mind of Christ	
Spiritual Timing	Spirit of Revival
Dynamics of Faith	The Champions of God
The Champions of God	The Ministry Gifts
Roots of Character	and much, much more!

You have a part — isn't it time you did something to reach the world for Jesus Christ? Send today for your application and catalog!

For more information or to receive a catalog and an application, please call (714) 661-3606 or write:

Spirit Life Bible College
P.O. Box 30710
Laguna Hills, CA 92654-0710

Discounts for couples and child care available